Elias Derby

The overland route to the Pacific

A report on the condition, capacity and resources of the Union Pacific and

Central Pacific railways

Elias Derby

The overland route to the Pacific
A report on the condition, capacity and resources of the Union Pacific and Central Pacific railways

ISBN/EAN: 9783337147716

Printed in Europe, USA, Canada, Australia, Japan

Cover: Foto ©Andreas Hilbeck / pixelio.de

More available books at **www.hansebooks.com**

The Overland Route to the Pacific.

A REPORT

ON THE

CONDITION, CAPACITY AND RESOURCES

OF THE

UNION PACIFIC

AND

CENTRAL PACIFIC RAILWAYS.

BY

E. H. DERBY, OF BOSTON.

October, 1869.

BOSTON:
LEE & SHEPARD, No. 149 WASHINGTON STREET.
1869.

Entered according to Act of Congress, in the year 1869,

By E. H. DERBY,

In the Clerk's Office of the District Court of the District of Massachusetts.

WRIGHT & POTTER, Printers, 79 Milk Street.

Messrs. Blake Bros. & Co.,

Bankers of Boston and New York:

Gentlemen:—At your suggestion, and through the kind permission of the President and Directors of the Union Pacific and Central Pacific Railroad Corporations, I have made inspection of their present condition, resources and capacity, and I have pleasure in stating that I have traversed the whole line of railways to and from the Atlantic to the Pacific Oceans, and carefully examined them on my way, travelling often on the rear platform, and stopping at the more important stations.

As some of the trade of Boston with the West now passes over the Vermont Central and a part of the Grand Trunk, I deemed it advisable to examine its line between Montreal and Detroit, and to pass over the Great Western, Michigan Central and Chicago and Northwestern Railways, on my way out, and to take the Hannibal and St. Joseph, C. B. and Quincy, Illinois Central, Great Western, and New York Central Lines on my return, and to draw parallels between some of them and the Pacific Lines. My investigations have been aided by the efficient staff you have given me, in Lord Cecil, from England, who has made English roads and engines a study, and has travelled much of the distance on the engines, and Mr. F. B. Blake, of the London House of Pixley, Abell, Langley and Blake, who accompanied me on the trip.

As other duties may deter me from making a more elaborate report, I submit to you a diary of our trip and the conclusions at which I have arrived.

I congratulate you and the country upon the despatch with which the Overland Railway has been finished, and the great expansion of business which must attend the completion of the Line.

Judiciously managed, with the telegraph on one hand and the express business on the other, and its sources of traffic well developed, I feel confident it will meet the hopes of its projectors and the expectations of the public.

Very respectfully,

E. H. DERBY.

Boston, Oct. 14th, 1869.

The Overland Route to the Pacific.

On the evening of August 9th, 1869, I left Boston for Montreal, accompanied by Mr. F. B. Blake. Our course is northerly by the Vermont Central Railway to the Grand Trunk at Montreal, from which point we propose to run to Chicago, following the course of the new interchangeable cars. We find a sleeping-car at the station, and after a pleasant night's run, awake the next morning at St. Albans.

August 10th.

We find a spacious and elegant station and a breakfast at St. Albans.

The train brings us to Montreal by 10, A. M., and we devote the day to the inspection of the tracks and stations of the Grand Trunk Railway. We call on Mr. Brydges and confer with the leading merchants of Canada, who give us a cordial reception, and inform us that trade is improving and exports and imports are larger than they were last year. I am happy to notice a change in the Grand Trunk since the summer of 1868. Its crippled cars have disappeared, and its track has improved, but it lacks a suitable depot at Montreal and a proper connection with tide-water. This deficiency must greatly impair its power to compete with steamers on the St. Lawrence. We learn, too, that the sections east of the river require renewal.* Mr. Brydges appreciates the importance of the Boston traffic, which

* See Appendix.

will be increased by branches now in progress to connect the Grand Trunk with lines through the Passumpsic and Amonoosac Valleys. He considers the changeable cars a decided success.

We dine with friends at the Club House.

WEDNESDAY, August 11th.

We leave Montreal at eight o'clock, A. M., for Toronto, and examine the line from the rear platform. Our average speed is twenty-one miles per hour, the location wide, the road direct, level and well ballasted, the bridges substantial, the depots of stone, with plats of flowers near them, but the iron, for at least a third of the way, is rough, and requires renewal. The country, until we pass Ogdensburg, is cold, flat and uninviting; the crops of oats and other grain backward; harvest not begun. As we pass Prescott the country improves, and we see fields of wheat and barley. Most of the crops must cross the road to reach the river.

The harvest here is beginning. The country is almost denuded of timber, but we notice piles of wood in the open air, with few or no wood-sheds to keep the wood dry, as on our American lines.

We notice few indications of local freight, but pass several freight trains, and reach Toronto, 333 miles from Montreal, at 12.40, A. M., just as a dinner-party, given to Sir Francis Hinckes, is dissolving, and we pass the guests on our way to our chambers. Their speeches, reported the next morn, favor the idea of independence, guaranteed by France and the United States. Do they think that Louis Napoleon may claim Quebec and the United States Ontario, when England retires, as she probably will, from this continent?

THURSDAY, August 12th.

We walk to the rolling-mill, so much discussed at the meetings of the Grand Trunk Railway Company, and from which came several car loads of rails that passed us yesterday; but the fires are out, and work suspended. We observe, however, many piles of splintered rails ready for the furnace.

As no train goes westerly until 11 o'clock, A. M., we walk with a friend, who pilots us through Toronto, a city of sixty thousand people, and notice its good streets, substantial structures and English aspect. In the markets we find abundance, and hear that contracts may be made by the year for the best pieces of beef, mutton and veal for ten cents the pound. We observe also, frequent notices of the Great Western line, which has been Americanized, and notice that its station is more spacious and attractive than that of the Grand Trunk.

The buildings of the Grand Trunk are chiefly of wood, and compared with those of the Great Western, are less attractive. At 11 o'clock, A. M., we start from the station with three cars and a hundred passengers, chiefly local, for they diminish as we proceed, and in seven hours we make Sarnia, above Detroit, leaving the oil wells to the left and their freight to the Great Western.

The road and the speed have both improved from yesterday, although the gradients rise to sixty feet. Some twenty miles require new iron. A little ballast is also wanted, but twenty thousand pounds would put the road in good condition; indeed, I am satisfied that a hundred and fifty thousand pounds judiciously expended between Montreal and Sarnia, on this, the best half of the Grand Trunk, would carry it above the level of our American lines, and enable trains to run thirty-five miles per hour and earn good dividends. The capacity of this line has been underrated, and it is deeply to be regretted that Mr. Brydges has not the means at his disposal to rival, if not surpass, the lines on the opposite side of the great lakes and river.

The location is a hundred feet in width, the bridges excellent, the banks well sloped and sodded. The ties, however, are of inferior wood, (oak, elm and hemlock,) and on the average, last but five years. We should discard the hemlock. The forests have been felled for fifty feet on each side of the line. Five section men keep eight miles in repair, and the line is very straight and level for long distances. We pass many piles of wood, but notice but few sheds for sawed wood, which in the moist climate of Canada must lead to a loss of fuel. We pass through a fine country, well cultivated, especially in the German towns of Guelph, Berlin, Breslau and Baden, where we notice many large stone barns and granaries. These are towns of three to eight thousand people, and remind me of Lancaster, Pennsylvania. There are men and women in the field. We see a few mowing and reaping machines, and notice fields of wheat, barley, oats, pease, flax and potatoes. Mr. Eliott, an intelligent Canadian, tells us that last year the crops were thirty per cent. below an average, this year twenty per cent. above one ; that this season wheat returns twenty-eight, barley thirty-five, pease thirty-five, and oats fifty bushels to the acre, and will afford a large surplus for exportation. This will flow to the railway. Wheat now sells for one dollar and ten cents, barley for seventy cents, and oats for forty cents per bushel. The repeal of the Treaty of Reciprocity depressed prices a fifth.

As respects independence, many favor it. In conversation, a majority take ground against a union with the States, but one of the most intelligent tells us that two bad seasons would lead to annexation.

At 6, P. M., we reach Sarnia, and after supper cross the ferry and take a car for Detroit, already nearly filled by a picnic party, apparently a low-priced one. The car is old, less than seven feet high, and by no means comfortable, but we run over a smooth and level line to Detroit, a city larger than Toronto, and late in the evening reach excellent quarters, at the Biddle House.

Thus far the Grand Trunk Railway has drawn little aid from its trade with Boston. A large portion of the freight over its branch to Portland goes by sea to Boston, but the circuit is so great, the transshipment, risk and delays so ruinous, that the line profits little from this part of its business. All this will be changed when the New Hampshire railways enter it, near the Canada line.

Then most of the freight now diverted by the Vermont Central will return to it, and the freight which now passes *via* Portland to Boston will become remunerative, for the goods may be sent through in one-third of the time which has of late been required.

Portland, where the Grand Trunk terminates, is a very spirited and ambitious city, but, when compared with Boston, sinks in importance.

Its population ranges from thirty to forty thousand, but within one hour of the Boston exchange there are seven hundred and fifty thousand people, and the wealth of Boston is rated for taxation at $549,000,000, while its annual sales, by the returns of the United States revenue, are more than fifty times as large as those of Portland.

It is the great centre of the manufactures of New England. Here its raw material is landed, and here a large portion of its goods are sold, and on the way from Montreal to Boston lies the valley of the Merrimac, studded with manufacturing cities. These might be supplied by the Grand Trunk with Western and Canadian produce.

It is now apparent that there was a serious error in the location of the Grand Trunk. It sprung from the ambition of Portland. It built the road with a broad gauge, to prevent a diversion to Boston. The result has injured the Grand Trunk, but Portland does not rival the commercial emporium of New England.

Again, the theory was, that the trade of Canada would be with England; but the Treaty of Reciprocity has demonstrated that New England is the great market of Canada, for here two-thirds of its exports were consumed, while England drew most of her grain and timber from the continent of Europe.

Boston receives most of its breadstuffs by the Boston & Albany line, which transports annually 1,400,000 tons, but charges high rates in consequence of its high gradients. It passes two ranges of mountains, and to obviate these the State is now making a tunnel of eight thousand yards, which will require several years for its completion; but there are no tunnels or heavy gradients over the route from Boston to Montreal, and the long levels of the Grand Trunk in the valley of the St. Lawrence give it great advantages.

When the Grand Trunk has a terminus at Boston, and Canadian independence carries free trade over the continent, we may well anticipate a development of its traffic which will revive the fainting hearts of its suffering stockholders.

Boston is the true terminus for the Grand Trunk line, for it has some advantages over both Portland and New York. Over Portland in the extent of its market, and the great resort of ships, which bring supplies for factories, and require return cargoes of produce. Over New York, because it is two hundred miles nearer Europe, and has a judiciary in whose hands property is secure, and merchants in whose stability and integrity the country confides.

Before it lies a brilliant future; it already wields the Union Pacific Railway, and must, ere long, have its lines of new steamers to connect China and Japan with Liverpool.

Eventually it will have a further impulse, from the Tunnel route, which will connect it with Lake Ontario, and from the Caughnawaga Canal, by means of which flour will be delivered from the great lakes at lower rates than the rates to New York.

DETROIT, August 13th.

After an excellent breakfast, on the white fish of the lakes, and a pleasant walk through the spacious avenues of Detroit, we take a view of its new city hall, an elegant edifice of freestone, and embark for Chicago at 9 1-2, A. M., in a car of the Michigan Central line, and make the run of 285 miles in eleven hours. Our average speed is nearly or quite forty miles the hour, exclusive of stops, but we are allowed ample time for dinner and supper. The train is in all its details the best I have ever seen,—the engine powerful and efficient. The train comprises five cars—a car for ladies and their attendants, a car for gentlemen, a second-class car, a smoking-car and a baggage-car, each long and airy, with a decked roof, patent springs and buffers, and suitable ventilators, and each can accommodate more than fifty passengers. An upper tier of windows runs along the decked roofs, and beside them are the ropes which communicate with the engineer and enable him to apply the brake to each car and stop the train within three lengths. A polite conductor walks with me from the rear platform to the baggage-room and gives me an arm-chair between its two wide doors, from which I get a fine view of the country on either side, and notice the aspect and varied agriculture of the country. The baggage-master tells me he has held his place since the road first opened, twenty years since, and has met with no accidents. His car runs as well as the ladies' car, and I write easily on my tablets.

The aspect of the country has changed since yesterday, although we have made little change in latitude.

The harvest has passed ; we notice less wheat-fields, more orchards, pastures, meadows and woodlands, and more Indian corn ; the country is more level and better adapted to grass.

With all respect for Mr. Brydges, we cannot but contrast the cars of yesterday, and especially that in which we finished our run to Detroit, on a hot summer eve, with the magnificent cars in which we travel to-day—lofty parlors or drawing-rooms on wheels. Our conductor thinks, from my description, that the car of last eve was one of the early cars of this line, now used for the emigrant train. The Grand Trunk line requires a better equipage. The trains from New York to Chicago now make the run of nine hundred and fifty miles in twenty-nine hours. It will not answer for Montreal to consume forty hours in running a less distance. She must expend a few thousands on her railways, introduce the Pullman and palace sleeping cars, and recollect that men who went out west in emigrant cars now return with their families as first-class passengers, and can appreciate and pay for comforts and luxuries.

We notice as we proceed that the bridges and masonry do not equal those of the Canadian lines, and that the corn crop, from an excess of moisture, is a failure. We notice, too, that while the sawed wood is kept dry in sheds, much wood before it is sawed is piled in the open air. This may answer under the sun of an American summer, but the wood must be dry when it reaches the furnaces or it wastes its strength that should create steam, in evaporating its own moisture.

We pass many pleasant towns of six to eight thousand inhabitants, many pleasant residences—Ann Arbor, with its university and twelve hundred students—and early in the evening reach Chicago, a city of three hundred thousand people, which prides itself on more than a dozen railways, and a port whose custom-house records more arrivals of tonnage, daily, than the custom-house of New York,—a port which receives, yearly, nearly three millions tons of lumber and breadstuffs, beside one or two millions of sheep, swine and cattle.

We meet with no detention on the Michigan Central Railway, although it dispatches on a single track thirty-six heavy trains daily, and the usual load of its freight trains of twenty-five cars exceeds two hundred tons. It is run by telegraph, and the conductor tells us its gain of income last year over the previous year was $200,000.

I regard it in most particulars a pattern line. Its average

charge for first-class through passengers is not far from two and a half cents per mile; its rates for freight very moderate.*

CHICAGO, August 14th.

We meet our young friend, Lord Cecil, at the Sherman House. He has returned to this point, with the party of scientific men who have been across the Mississippi to Des Moines, to observe the eclipse, and as it is now Friday eve, and we cannot reach Omaha, the eastern terminus of the Union Pacific line, except by travelling on Sunday, we determine to devote a day to Chicago.

SATURDAY, August 14th.

We have a letter to Mr. Chesborough, the city engineer, and I find in him an old acquaintance. We accept his invitation to inspect the public works. The city is actively engaged in improvements. Its original level was too low for perfect drainage, and the city has raised it, in the last ten years, eight or ten feet, taking up the original buildings to the new level. It has carried out a tunnel two miles under Lake Michigan, to procure pure water, and is deepening the Illinois Canal through a long cut in rock, to turn part of the waters of Lake Michigan through its river into the Illinois, to purify its harbor and improve navigation. The waters of the lakes will thus find a new outlet at New Orleans.

The growth of its navigation, and the frequent passage of vessels through its drawbridges, have also induced the city to construct a tunnel under the river for both foot passengers and carriages; and such has been its success that another has been commenced within a few weeks after the completion of the first.

With an assistant engineer, we visit the river tunnel. It commences on a street leading to the river, half way between two bridges, eight hundred feet apart, at a point where the river is two hundred feet in width. Like the Salem Tunnel, it has

* See Appendix.

open approaches, one four hundred feet, the other three hundred feet in length, and the whole extent of tunnel and approaches is sixteen hundred feet. Its depth below the level of the street is forty-one feet. Its height "in the clear" is fifteen feet, and it has sixteen feet of water over it.

. The gradient is very easy; on one side one foot is sixteen, on the other, one is eighteen. There are separate arches for the carriages going each way, and a sidewalk for passengers. It has cost $400,000, and is taken by the passengers in preference to the bridges. In winter, I presume it will be easy to keep the temperature low, and to coat the floors with snow, when snow is blown from the bridges.

Chicago presents wide avenues lined with fine houses and churches, and some immense magazines of merchandise.

In one of them, the warehouse of Field, Lester & Co., where we call, with letters, the annual sales reach fifteen millions of dollars.

As we traverse the city we purchase grapes and pears that have arrived in good order from California. In the course of the morning we visit a warehouse used for the sale of cars and materials for railways. We find there has been at the West, where long and level routes have been opened, a strong tendency to increase the size, weight and cost of passenger cars, and to improve their quality; the best cars, like the best hotels, are most attractive, and one line cannot afford to be outdone by a rival line. Cars are now built sixty-six feet in length, costing sixteen thousand dollars. There are three classes of these cars. The Pullman Sleeping Car, the Palace or Saloon Car, for day use, and the Dining Car; and here I examine a Pullman car. I have given the length and cost. The width is ten feet, the height of the interior ten feet six inches, and height of exterior fourteen feet four inches; the chief materials, black walnut, plated ware, embossed French plate glass and mirrors.

As you enter you pass a wash-room, with marble table and

bowl, a commodious water-closet and state-room at each end. Then settees on either side for two persons each, with ample space between, and sloping sides· to the sloping and frescoed ceiling which rises to a long decked roof, panelled, with windows. Large plate glass windows and curtains line the sides. At night the sloping roof comes down, with frames, bedding and curtains, and forms two ranges of berths, forty inches wide, much more commodious than the berths of the Cunard steamers, and so few are the jerks, and so steady the movements of these cars, and so great the facilities for change of position, that you travel with little or no fatigue, and sleep nearly as well as in your own chamber. By ten o'clock, P. M., the lamps suspended under the decks are extinguished, and the guard devotes the night in the wash-room to brushing boots and clothes. Ice-water may always be drawn from a silver faucet, and fruit, newspapers and sometimes sandwiches may be bought from a tidy news-boy, who comes in during the daytime.

The extra charge for these cars varies in the West from one dollar and a half to four dollars per night and day.

In the Saloon Car revolving arm-chairs are furnished, with cozy state-rooms for two or four persons, in long aisles with plate windows of forty inches in diameter, and many ornaments and comforts.

In the Dining Cars meals are ordered, and the travellers are served with the best viands the country affords at fair prices.

Thus the traveller, by adding half a cent or a cent a mile to his fare, commands comforts and luxuries, and makes travelling a pleasure.

There is one drawback to the satisfaction given by these cars: it is the additional weight of such large structures. Formerly, a car to seat fifty passengers weighed less than ten tons, and cost but two thousand dollars, and to-day, in our paper currency, would cost but three thousand dollars; but the palatial cars I have described, weigh twenty-four to twenty-eight tons. Each

Pullman car has twenty-eight berths, many of which accommodate two persons. And the extra charge, if not diverted from the road by intervening companies, more than suffices to pay for the additional cost of traction. I dwell upon these cars, as we are to see few others before our return to Chicago.

In the afternoon we make several excursions through this city, now some seven miles in length, and four or five in breadth. We visit some of its new parks and vast cattle yards, where in the busy days of autumn, fifteen thousand head of cattle, as many sheep, and one hundred and fifty thousand swine are sometimes congregated.

In the evening we learn that intense competition has reduced freights between Chicago and the Atlantic seaboard to the rate of seven dollars per ton. A long continuance of such rates cannot be expected. They are little more than one-third the rates now claimed for half the distance by the new lines from Chicago to Omaha.

SUNDAY, August 15th.

We attend the Episcopal Church, on Wabash Avenue. In the course of the day, Senators Morrill and Patterson, and several members of Congress arrive in an express train of Pullman cars, with a saloon and dining car, bringing their ladies with them. We are joined also by Messrs. Atkins and Prentiss, of Boston, in thirty-two hours from Philadelphia. The two last propose to accompany us to Cheyenne, on their way to Colorado.

In the afternoon we walk to the passenger-house of the Michigan Southern and Rock Island Railways. It is of block stone, four hundred and fifty feet in length by one hundred and eighty feet in width, with roof projecting on each side over the sidewalk. It would cover six such houses as we found at the Montreal station. These great Western lines, however, are outgrowing their stations. They must soon be enlarged.

At 9 o'clock, P. M., we part with Senators Morrill and Sherman, and take passage by the Chicago & North-western line, *via*

Clinton, for Omaha. Distance, four hundred and eighty-eight miles; the fare, twenty dollars for each person. We pay also five dollars for a saloon with three berths.

Our car is a Pullman car, with the latest improvements. We reserve a sofa for our clothes, and retire early and sleep until we approach Cedar Rapids, beyond the Mississippi, and 220 miles from Chicago, and are notified to dress for breakfast. After our repast, we take a day car, for the residue of our day's journey.

MONDAY, August 16th.

We are now running 267 miles from Cedar Rapids to the Missouri, at Omaha, across the young State of Iowa, one of the most fertile in the Union and fast filling with people.

Our train carries some sixty passengers. The travellers for Omaha divide at Chicago, and as three railways are already made, and four more are in progress, to connect the great lakes and Mississippi River with the Union Pacific Railway, rates must fall to the Eastern level, as seven lines will compete for the traffic.

We look from the rear platform on a fine country; no waste lands, but fields of wheat, corn, oats, or open prairies. As we advance, the crops, especially those of corn, improve, but as we approach the frontier the value of land gradually falls from $30 to $5 or $10 per acre, and we find less cultivation and improvement; the settlers have just reached the western line of Iowa, advancing with the railways, and have met there the tide which has flowed up the Missouri into Nebraska.

We pass coal mines on our way, with veins of bituminous coal, which comes out in square blocks, but soon disintegrates. It is of impure character, but answers for locomotives, and sells for about three dollars at the pits, where two hundred tons are delivered daily.

It has been carried to Omaha, where it meets the coal from

Wyoming. But the Wyoming coal, at ten dollars, has the preference.

We regret to find that this section of the North-western line has suffered much from the wet season and the carriage of materials for the Pacific line. Many of the rails require removal. The road-bed, but seven to nine feet in width, requires a large amount of ballast. Our conclusions are verified by the fact, that while the Pacific trains have run on time, and the New York trains have run in twenty-nine hours to Chicago, the trains on this line have been irregular, after requiring twenty-nine hours for half the distance from New York to Chicago. At the present moment, each of the lines running easterly from Omaha towards the seaboard, the C. & N. Western, the Rock Island and the St. Joseph's and Council Bluffs, require ballast, and the one which first obtains it will have the preference.

We cross the Missouri by ferry, and reach Omaha in the evening.

Large steamers now convey passengers and cars laden with freight across the river, and connect with rails laid across the intervales of the river. The charge for passage is three-fourths of a dollar for passengers, and ten dollars per car for freight, and the change involves a loss of one or two hours in making the connection. A bridge is in progress, resting on iron tubes driven through the shifting sands of the Missouri. It will be of great service, and has become absolutely necessary, since a rival line has obtained a bridge at Kansas City. The new bridge is to be built by an independent company, to whose stock the lines centering at Omaha and Council Bluffs contribute.

Tuesday, August 17th.

After a pleasant night's rest at the hotel, I rise at 6, A. M., for my journal and an early breakfast.

Rival cities are rising near the Bluffs, on each side of the

Missouri. They are four miles apart, for ample space must be given to the rapid and capricious river. Omaha, on the west bank, has at least sixteen thousand people, and Council Bluffs more than half that number, and the bridge and railway will unite them. Each position is good, but Omaha has most capital and people, and the current of opinion sets in its favor, as most western cities rise on the western shores of the great rivers, although Memphis and Quincy are exceptions.

The lines from the East will plant most of their stations on the eastern shore, and the Union Pacific will probably place there a union depot, but its shops and warehouses will be chiefly on the west bank of the Missouri.

The Union Pacific Railway begins at Omaha, and its directors have been fortunate in securing the services of Colonel Hammond and his associates, Messrs. Nichols and Mead, to manage the railway. All speak of them as men of ability and experience, " as the right men, in the right place."

After an interview with these gentlemen, in which we gain much valuable information, we repair to the yards and workshops of the company, and devote to them the residue of the day. Here is a large stock of engines, cars, wheels, tires, axles and other materials, and piles of scrap iron, which accumulated while the road was in progress. Steel tires are in general use, and highly approved. The engines are from the best builders, of large size and in good condition. In the car-shop, new passenger cars are in progress. For the moment, the line is overstocked with freight cars. It has 160 engines, 80 long passenger and mail cars, and 3,000 freight cars, and employs 250 of the latter on connecting lines, at a rent of $11,000 per month.

We call at the land office and confer with Mr. Davis, the land agent, who exhibits the plans and surveys.

The land of the company comprises the alternate sections for twenty miles on each side of the line, or 12,800 acres per mile.

From this must be deducted the land previously granted or occupied, which will reduce the grant to about twelve millions of acres—a part of it of great fertility, on the lower sections of the Platte; a part in pastures above it; a part in alkali land; a part abounds in coal and other minerals. The land, at the estimate of Mr. Davis, ranges from 20 cents to $20 per acre, and in his opinion will average more than a dollar and a half per acre. His sales are at the rate of $150,000 per month, and average between five and six dollars per acre. He is now selling the most fertile and accessible land, but expresses the belief that as emigrants pour in the land will advance in value.

During the day, we discuss the great questions of freight and fare, and find the officers of the line inclined to favor moderate prices. In the course of our inquiries, we find the road has on hand nearly sixty thousand cords of wood, costing ten dollars a cord, surplus lumber, rails, tools, wheels and other materials designed for the extension of the line; that it has also a large claim against the Central Pacific, for fifty-six miles of road-bed and track it has finished west of Ogden, and find these, with a balance of two and a fourth millions coming from the government, approach eight millions of dollars.

Here is a fund to close up contracts, to complete structures adapted to present use, but requiring further outlay for completion.

The superintendent has just reduced the tariff on coal from Carbon to Omaha, a distance of six hundred and fifty miles, to $10 per ton, so that coal is now sold at Omaha for $12 per ton, or half the price that good coal commanded the last winter.

From Carbon to a point near Cheyenne, the first hundred and fifty miles, there is but one rise to be surmounted which exceeds thirty-five feet per mile, and that is at Sherman, five hundred and fifty miles from Omaha, where the gradient is eighty-six feet to the mile. At Sherman the train is 8,230 feet above the level of the sea, and 7,300 feet above Omaha, and finds a gradual descent on the way to Omaha, except one ascending gradient of thirty-five feet, at Archer, near Sherman, and two of twenty-nine and thirty-three feet near Omaha, which together are less than ten miles in length.

No railway yet built presents a route better adapted for the transmission of coal. With its advantage in greater length and but one lading and unlading for 656 miles, it surpasses the Reading Railway in its power to transport coal.

It is not at Carbon alone that the line commands coal, but for nearly four hundred miles, between the Laramie Basin and Evanston, there is abundance of coal, often cropping out by the roadside, and at Evanston, sixty-eight miles east of Ogden, a vein of thirty feet has been opened, of superior quality.

At Carbon, the vein is eight feet thick, and is within the location of the line. Here one hundred and twenty tons are delivered daily from a shaft but eighty feet deep. The coal is light, and resinous; it burns with a bright flame, forms no clinker, and often shows small balls of resin, but no traces of sulphur are visible, and it is very popular as fuel.

The coal is held by the Wyoming Coal Company, but the vice-president assures us that more than nine-tenths of the stock of the Wyoming Company is held in trust for the Union Pacific.

WEDNESDAY, August 18th.

After a day devoted to Omaha, we start on the Union Pacific Line at 9, A. M. Messrs. Hammond & Nichols meet us at the station and present us with a map and profile of the route, giving topography, heights, grades and distances, also a license to mount the engine, and we launch upon the prairies. Our train comprises a mail car, baggage car, smoking car, two excellent passenger cars, and two Pullmans, each sixty-five feet long, and each having berths to accommodate thirty-five passengers, which give place to a long saloon and padded sofas in the daytime, with wash-rooms at either end, and a tank of ice-water, with its silver faucet, is always accessible. The saloons shine with polished black walnut, silver plate, mirrors, plate glass, and costly lamps are suspended from the frescoed roof, ten feet above the floor.

We assemble on the rear platform, and are soon joined by an engineer and two contractors, who have built many railways, on their way across the plains.

For two days' use of the Pullman cars and berths, we each pay eight dollars, and on the average, a dollar for each meal. The cars are furnished by the Pullman Company, who pay the three servants in charge and keep the interior of the cars in repair; while the railway takes care of the exterior and divides the income.

One of the Eastern lines failed to connect with us; we have but seventy passengers and ample space for our comfort, as we could easily seat two hundred.

The emigrant train has this morning gone forward with seven hundred passengers, charged $50 each, from sea to sea; while the rate for first-class is $150 from New York to the Pacific.

As we launch out on the prairie, we notice two telegraph lines: one with three wires, owned by the Western Union Company, the other with two wires, the property of the railway. These lines extend from Omaha to the Pacific.

As we proceed, we notice windmills at the water stations, propelled by the winds which blow across the plains, which pump the water, and on either side land of great fertility, fast improving. No forests, a few cottonwood trees along the streams, but young groves of apple trees, walnuts and cottonwood springing up around the settlers' houses. Meadows, cornfields and wheat fields. The native grasses would make several tons of hay to the acre, but a small portion is yet mowed or pastured. The corn is more luxuriant than any we have seen, and the crop will be a good one.

In the course of the day we pass Fort Kearney, and by 10 P. M. the North Platte River. For this distance the rail is laid without fish joints, two to three feet above the plain. The road-bed is ten feet wide, with ties whose centres are two feet apart, and is ballasted chiefly with the sand that underlies the soil, resembling that which the Platte River rolls into sand bars. It gives a firm bed for the rail, but is liable to yield to wind and rain and would be greatly improved by a layer of gravel. As the rail wears out and the ties, in part of cottonwood, decay, it will be politic to raise the track by gravel, as this will secure the ballast, avoid freshets and reduce the annual charge for repairs. But for a new line, it is to-day in excellent condition, and our motion easy and equable.

We dine and sup in commodious rooms near the track, and at night the berths and bedding descend from the sloping roof, and we sleep comfortably in our state rooms, on mattresses forty inches wide. During the evening, when three hundred miles from Omaha, we converse with a gentleman who had been thirty days afoot on the plains, in achieving the same distance we have traversed since breakfast. The cars move quietly, and stop and start without jar; we sleep quite as well as at sea, and are refreshed by our slumbers.

THURSDAY, August 19th.

We are called at 6.30 A. M., to dress for breakfast at Cheyenne, some miles beyond us. This station is five hundred and sixteen miles from Omaha, and five thousand feet above it. Some of the passengers point out deer and antelope in the distance, and occasional herds of cattle, but the buffalo avoid the railway, and have no ear for the music of the engine. We pass a few detachments of troops at the chief stations, but see one Indian only hunting with his bow and arrow. We are now travelling on a well gravelled road, and on a good rail laid with fish joints, the road-bed improves as we approach the mountains; while the grass is browner and less luxuriant than at lower levels. The sunflower grows luxuriantly in the ditch on each side of the railway, and the air is exhilarating.

After breakfast we begin to ascend the chief rise between the two oceans,—young Cecil on the engine; and in twenty-eight miles, with a gradient of seventy-nine feet to the mile, reach Sherman, 8,235 feet above the sea, and descend with a short gradient of eighty-six feet to Laramie, 573 miles from Omaha, which we reach at noon. The chief summit at Sherman is passed without a tunnel, by a very judicious location through cuts of fifteen to thirty feet in depth in limestone, slate and decomposed granite, which affords good material for ballasting the track in the plains below. A single engine, with a little aid at Cheyenne, might take down seven hundred tons at once and distribute it upon the plains, and thus perfect the road-bed and prolong the life of the rails, now in excellent condition, and costly to renew. The embankments are light, the route well chosen, and the passage of the mountains, now free from snow, does credit to the engineer. The line of perpetual snow is still five thousand feet above us.

As Laramie is an important station, on a plateau seven thousand feet above the sea, and we are now on the table land of the continent, which, for five hundred miles, ranges from six to seven thousand feet above tide-water, until the line reaches the Echo and Weber canons, and descends nearly two thousand feet to the level of Salt Lake City, we determine to alight and devote a day to the shops and surroundings of Laramie.

We dine on antelope and other choice viands at an excellent hotel, erected by the company, where two hundred passengers may easily dine, and sixty find comfortable lodgings. This hotel is already a favorite resort for invalids who wish to inhale the pure mountain air.

We present a letter of introduction to Dr. Latham, who has charge of a hospital for employees, and I am indebted to him for much valuable information and a meteorological journal which I hope to subjoin to this Report. He takes us to his garden to show us that pease, beans, potatoes and tomatoes grow well at this elevation, and he presents us with luxuriant stalks of oats, barley and wheat, which grew up beside an old warehouse at Benton, on this plateau, from grain dropped there accidentally.

He considers this region and the hills and higher plains well adapted to pasturage, and assures us that cattle will thrive summer and winter in natural pastures without folds or shelter.

To illustrate this he gives the case of a farmer who came to these plains four years since, with seven hundred sheep, that have increased to twenty-eight hundred, and quotes Mr. Major, who has sent many thousand trains across the plains, and found that cattle and sheep will thrive in the open air, both on the plains and hills on the whole territory from Mexico to British America.

How is it, that with beef selling at thirty-five cents a pound in Boston, and with statisticians reporting that the people of Great Britain eat but two ounces of meat a day, that these great pastures, within three days of Boston and fourteen days of Liverpool, are not covered with cattle?

In the afternoon we go through the engine-house and find stalls for twenty engines, and examine the shops of the company, which are provided with lathes, tools, tires and other materials for repairs.

We inspect the coal in use on the road and find it very resinous and very acceptable to the engine-men.

One of the employees tells me the trains were detained last winter for several weeks between Laramie and Salt Lake, but thinks the danger may be averted by three miles of sheds, over exposed cuts, and by snow-fences, some of which are now completed. The foreman of the shops tells me, their engines with eight drivers are competent to take one hundred and sixty tons of coal over the summit. With such power, two trains from Carbon, with three hundred tons of coal, may be taken with one assistant engine over the summit, and then drawn by one engine to the first ascending grade near Omaha. The returning coal trains can take back the cars with freight from the East, which now exceeds the freight from the West.

FRIDAY, August 20th.

We take breakfast this morning with passengers who came by a train from California, which brings a hundred and thirty people. This train must pay at least $13,000 to the two railways. It arrives on time by the card.

After breakfast, we ride out upon the plains with Dr. Latham, who entertained us hospitably last eve at his residence. We find good grass, and notice in many places the bones and wallows of buffalo, who frequented these pastures. During our drive, a flock of plover light within gun-shot, and we see a wild duck sailing along the Laramie River, within shooting distance.

We find a flock of five hundred Mexican sheep that have wintered on the plains, in good condition, and pass by the inclosure where they are folded at night, and a herd of cattle that supply the hotel with beef and milk. They are feeding on dry grass on the high ground and in meadows near the river.

Dr. Latham makes the annual fall of rain in this country but twelve inches. We have had as much fall in a single storm in New England, and carry away roads and bridges, which are here secure.

At 12½, P. M., after an early dinner, we again take the cars for the West, and in the evening pass Carbon, and stop to examine the mine, where a train of cars is receiving the coal from the pits' mouth, on a side track. The coal, as it comes from the mines, confirms our favorable impressions. Doubtless more mines will be opened; but the mines at Carbon and Evanston alone will supply the entire line with coal at an average cost of $4.00 to $5.00 per ton at the points of consumption in a country nearly destitute of wood. Nature, by this bountiful supply, has placed a mighty lever in the hands of the Union Pacific. From the bridge across the North Platte, we find the road well made, the track laid with fish joints and in good condition.

SATURDAY, August 21st.

At 3 o'clock this morn I awake and find the track less smooth than yesterday; it was laid with great dispatch during the winter and early spring. After the embankment was finished the sides were thrown up for ballast and the track laid on this surface, and now a steam shovel, and Mormons, with oxen attached to large scrapers, are busy ballasting the line. We pass a number of trestle bridges, gravel trains and viaducts where the alkaline stone, used for abutments, has crumbled, and a large force is engaged in perfecting these structures, and we pass in safety through the beautiful scenery of Echo and Weber canons, wonderful ravines, pass several small tunnels, one lined with timber, others self-supporting, and the immense rocks, Great Eastern and Western. The train passes the one-thousandth mile-stone in forty-nine hours from Omaha, running slowly over the new road. A dozen passengers gather upon the platform as we descend to Uintah, where we alight and take the coach for Salt Lake City late in the forenoon.

All the contractors and engineers with whom we have travelled, agree that the line, for a new road, is in excellent condition, and those who have seen the Illinois Central and the Ohio lines in their infancy, think this superior to them when first opened, and able to run with much greater speed.

In the coach all distinctions of rank are lost; the Mormons secure the best seats. Young Cecil sits next to a baker from London, and another Englishman, quite unpolished, finds fault with both countries.

The road is rough, and we are glad to stop to change horses at a Mormon inn, and here we notice the ravages of the grasshopper. They have devoured the pease, beans and lettuce, and assailed the peaches and apples of the garden, and stripped many of the fruit-trees. They have destroyed some of the leaves of the corn; but the great army have left the wheat and vineyards uninjured.

In the mild climate of this region, wheat and corn ripen early, the grain has been harvested, the corn is beyond the reach of frost, and grapes, pears, peaches and apples are ripening. The trees show smooth bark and vigorous growth. I trace the luxuriant vegetation, not to mere irrigation, but to the quickening power of alkali, dissolved in water, which has converted the sage bush into luxuriant orchards and cornfields.

The wheat, without fertilizers, returns this year, thirty-four bushels to the acre, and the cost of irrigation does not exceed twelve dollars per acre. The annual cost of maintenance is less than one-fifth of this amount. How much less would it cost to create a farm in the forest?

As we approach Salt Lake we pass over plains and through valleys and farms covered with brown grass or sage brush, and many spots exhibiting signs of alkali. Sometimes the effervescence is visible, and in some places the water is discolored, but now we find ourselves in a large basin, with the lake before us, terraces, surrounded by mountains, which by their shape remind one of Vesuvius. We pass rills from the mountains, crossing our road and led to terraces below us, on which the reapers are now harvesting the golden grain.

Our route is along the edge of the wheat fields for nearly thirty miles, to Salt Lake City, which extends in a succession of terraces or fields of different levels, towards the lake, and presents a charming appearance. It is laid out in lots of an acre and a quarter, cultivated as gardens, containing small but tasteful houses. These gardens are irrigated from the hills. Apples, pears, peaches, plums and grapes grow luxuriantly in these inclosures. Water has clothed the sombre pastures and sage-bush plains with trees and verdure, and produced results which water fails to produce on our eastern soil.

The young trees grow with a smooth bark, which reminds me of trees washed with soap-suds; and a few days later I notice the same aspect on the plains of California, where fruit-trees have been planted on plains impregnated with alkali.

Is it not possible that the alkali dissolved in water is the secret agent of this remarkable vegetation, and that the wastes now branded by travellers as worthless, will eventually be transformed by the magic power of water, to gardens, orchards and wheat fields,—that reservoirs will be made in mountain ravines, and conduits laid to carry the water across the basins, and that the growth of trees will increase the rain-fall?

Since the settlement of the Mormons in this valley, twenty years since, the rain-fall has increased, and already on the Pacific route showers are more frequent than when the hunter first crossed the mountains.

We pass the Sulphur Spring, memorable for the death of Robinson, the old and new tabernacles, the houses of Brigham Young and his chief followers, pass through wide streets with rivulets and shade-trees on either side, and alight at the chief hotel, the Townsend House, where we are entertained by Mr. Townsend and his three helpmates, and where we are soon after joined by the congressional party.

I present a letter to Mr. Hooper, a Mormon member of Congress, and devote the afternoon to the city, and the evening to the theatre, where we see several wives and children of Brigham Young, and the elite of the city.

Mr. Hooper, the Mormon member of Congress, tells us that the Mormons are a peaceful people, but does not seek to extenuate the death of Robinson.

He tells us all the nails which were driven in the Mormon

houses have cost thirty-five cents a pound for transportation, but thinks the railway, which reduces that cost to *five*, charges too high. He is disappointed because the railway does not reach the city, and thinks it will injure the trade of Utah, which found a market in the emigration across the plains.

SUNDAY, August 22d.

Rose at 6, A. M. The clear sky, gardens and scenery of this city bring Italy before me, and the blue mountains which encircle it, and lake in the distance, remind me constantly of the environs of Naples.

The Mormons have shown good taste in their selection of this magnificent valley.

At 10, A. M., we repair to the old tabernacle, a structure of elliptic shape, which will hold fifteen hundred, and is well filled. An organ and choir are in a gallery at one end, and the elders, grey-headed men, occupy a platform at the other. Elder Rockwell opens the meeting. He calls on Elder Boise, who has just returned from Virginia, to give an account of his mission. Elder Boise addresses the people as the Latter Day Saints, tells them "he went at the call of the President, and left them with reluctance, but found an opening in Wythe County, Virginia, and in some of the inland counties of North Carolina, where the soil was poor, the people poor, and the land set edgewise, and they had to till it on both sides; that he found there that slavery had been a failure, the rebellion a failure, emancipation a failure, and their religion a failure; that some women in this city thought their lot a hard one, but he had seen white women follow the plough; that he told them of the House the Lord had established in the mountains for his saints; that they alone followed the Bible; that they alone had apostles, bishops and seventy elders, and had fulfilled prophecy; that Providence had sent them water in dry places, and in one place a hundred and fifty springs had broken out where they had never flowed before; that a minister who had turned them from his door in a rain had died soon afterwards, and a church from which they were excluded had been struck by lightning; and that he had brought home a train of followers." Thus do they beguile the poor and unhappy. He added, "that the love for one wife was not lost in the love for the second, any more than the love for a first child was lost in love for a second; that they did not put one woman on a pedestal to worship her, but saved the sex from degradation."

When I looked at the array of homely women before me, I came to the conclusion that if they each had but one-fourth of a husband, they would have but one-fourth of a chance in the outer world. I could discover no beatitude in their expression. They were clad as plainly as they looked, and the contrast between them and the gentile ladies who visited them was very marked and striking.

Elder Cannon also addressed the meeting. He told them "they were driven to this valley by their foes, and thanked them for it; that if they left it they would find corrupt men in the world, and would be glad to return; that they could not be driven from it by the red hand of violence; that plurality of wives would not be abandoned; that you might strike off the head of the mustard, but the seed would be scattered; that they accepted the consequences of the sacrifices they had made;" to which the people responded with several loud amens.

In the afternoon we visit the new tabernacle, like the other, elliptic or egg-shaped in its form, and large enough to hold five thousand people. At one end is an organ of immense size, built by the Mormons, and estimated to cost $100,000.

The elders occupy a raised platform, and some of them break and distribute bread among the audience. The elder, Elrigo, makes a prayer, a hymn is sung, a missionary reports his success in converting many poor people at Southampton, England, who have come with him to the valley, and George Smith, the historian of the sect, recounts their adventures at Nauvoo, their flight to Council Bluffs, and their establishment in this valley, where their settlements extend for six hundred miles over plains once covered by sage bush or alkali, where they raise grain, corn, cotton and fruit.

He tells us the crickets once came in armies to devour their crops, but were destroyed by a remarkable flight of sea-gulls, from the lake. After the audience is dismissed, the members of Congress ascend the platform and are presented to Brigham Young.

During the evening, Messrs. Young, Cannon, and Smith call upon the guests at the Salt Lake House, and I am introduced to them. I learn from them that a branch railway to Ogden is nearly graded and will be completed by October; that they have nearly finished a canal thirty-five miles in length, thirty feet wide and four feet in depth, partly for irrigation and partly to extend the navigation of the lake, and that by the railway, lake and canal, they will send goods to the interior. They have constructed nearly four hundred miles of the Pacific Railway.

I asked Mr. Cannon how he explained the miracle of one hundred and fifty springs. He said in one of their townships, they had a stream which they supposed would water two hundred acres, but it sufficed for several tracts of land, and when they were saturated, the water broke out in springs below them and watered the next terrace, and thus they had reclaimed five thousand acres in one locality. I then inquired if they followed the injunctions of St. Paul and confined their bishops to one wife, and if, like the Greek Church, they forbid them to take a second, when the first one died. To which with a smile he replied, we construe St. Paul's words to mean that "the bishop must have at least one wife." This, I replied, is what we lawyers term a very liberal construction.

We learn from these visitors that the lake has risen eleven feet since the Mormons entered the valley; that the climate becomes more moist as cultivation advances, and that the alkali is utilized to make soap and is used as a substitute for saleratus.

The city of Salt Lake has sixteen thousand people, and the Territory one hundred and twenty thousand, nearly all Mormons. A post of the United States, with several hundred troops is planted near them. It now pays twenty-two dollars a ton for coal, and will be aided by the railway.

I venture to predict that on the completion of the railway, the coal from Evanston will supply the Mormon territory and this military station. That coal alone will support a daily train, and it would not surprise me if it should carry wood and lumber also, as well as goods, and return laden with salt, to which the Mormons may easily reduce the dense waters of the lake.

MONDAY, August 23d.

At 5 o'clock, A. M., after an early breakfast on the salmon trout of Utah, we take our seats in the coach. Some forty passengers are on the wing, after passing the Sunday at Salt Lake; and fill three coaches. On our way an intelligent farmer tells us that although irrigated land is worth a hundred dollars an acre in Utah, and the crops are large, the farms are smaller and less profitable than those of Iowa. He concedes, however, that they yield more wheat and fruit per acre.

We learn from him that coal rose last winter to $40 a ton at Salt Lake, and that the scarcity of fuel has been a great drawback to the Mormons. On our way to Uintah we catch many glimpses of the lake and wheat fields and surrounding mountains. At Uintah we find the cars on time, and at 11.30 A. M. join, for the third time, a train for California. At Ogden, four miles west of Uintah, we pass the Salt Lake Branch and future terminus of the Union Pacific. At Corinne we cross Bear River, an important stream, on which logs and ties may be floated three hundred miles to the lake, where timber now sells for $45 per thousand. It would be desirable for the Union Pacific, when it settles with the Central line, to secure the transportation of this freight at low rates to Ogden.

Beyond Ogden the Union Pacific has laid its track 56 miles to Promontory, a high peninsula jutting into the lake, and has graded thirty-five miles more westward, while the Central Pacific has graded some fifteen miles east of Promontory. Thus have the two companies invested in earthworks two or three hundred thousand dollars in their contest for supremacy. It may be hoped these road-beds may some day be utilized for second tracks; for the present the investment is dormant.

At Promontory the two lines meet, but no station greets the passenger; the precise point for the station is not yet fixed, and the operatives of the two companies, Chinese on one side and Hibernians on the other, like two hostile armies, are still encamped under canvass. An early decision as to the point of union, and suitable stations, are important to both parties.

The present spot is not fit for a station. Water is now drawn to it, twenty miles on one side and fifteen on the other, but at Ogden or Corinne, and at other points, pure water is easily accessible. The whole line of the Union Pacific from Omaha to Ogden is now well supplied with both coal and water, and in future it will draw its ties from St. Paul's to Columbus and Omaha, or from Bear River to Ogden, at a cost that will not probably exceed sixty-five cents each, and find a portion of its supplies at similar rates on the North Platte or Green River.

After shifting baggage and thus losing two hours at Promontory, we enter the silver palace cars of the Central Pacific. Our train comprises two silver palace, two passenger and two baggage or mail cars, with about one hundred first-class passengers, and we take the berths we have engaged by telegraph. In ascending the short gradient of eighty feet or more, at Promontory, we have used two engines and crossed a trestle bridge—strong, but a temporary structure.

The last sixty miles have been made hastily by a large body of men, who have temporarily used the side of the embankments for surfacing, and some work is still required for completion.

The cars in which we move are very tasteful and commodious; less costly, but almost as elegant, while they are lighter, than those of the Union line. The road bed of the Central line is wide, and all but thirty-five miles of it appears to be well ballasted with gravel.

Its curvature, however, is ten degrees, in place of six, on the Union line, and as it clings in many places to the foot hills, its gradients occasionally rise to 70 feet. We cannot fully appreciate the views of the engineer in his choice of routes, as a more level line might have been run through the valley. He may have had in view a better supply of water from the hills; the track is smooth, the rails fish jointed, and we move on pleasantly and equably across several basins fringed with mountains, towards the valley of the Humboldt.

Here, in lake and river, are lasting memorials of the great philosopher of Europe and explorer of the new world.

TUESDAY, August 24th.

We are now running through mountain passes and the valley of the Humboldt, and stop to breakfast at Elcho, opposite the mining districts of Cope and White Pine.

The platform of the station is thronged by miners, and boys offer us fruit and papers at high prices. The currency now changes from paper to gold, and we pay five dollars each for our berths and a quarter of a dollar for a paper, while our meals cost us usually a dollar. The track continues uniformly good, but the fuel piled by the wayside, consists of small cedar wood, and does not compare with that piled on the line of the Union Pacific. Since we entered the Central Pacific the trackmen are Chinese, apparently quiet and industrious, and the slopes and ditches evince much care and patient industry.

The track is in fine condition. We pass occasional meadows, herds of cattle and hay fields, that have been mown, but most of the country is covered with dry grass or sage bush and wears a sombre aspect.

At eve, we stop at Humboldt for our dinner, and here we notice a conduit from the mountain which brings water and fertility.

In front of our inn is a garden, just reclaimed from the waste; the sage bush still stands around it, and a belt of it crosses the garden, but "kind nature's sweet restorer," the rill from the mountain, has called into life corn, potatoes, pease, beans and other vegetables, and given proof of latent fertility on these wide-spread plains. We hear too of green valleys among the distant hills, and that cattle will thrive on the dry pasture.

We learn that at three points on the Central line water is taken in tanks to stations, but that soon all will come from the mountain springs in pipes, some of which will exceed nine miles in length.

No part of the line will suffer from an insufficient supply of water.

During the night, we pass Humboldt Lake and enter the valley of the Truckee, a mountain stream that flows from Lake Taho, on the borders of California.

WEDNESDAY, August 25th.

At 4, A. M., I discern pine trees from my window, and rise to watch our course over the Sierra Nevada, whose eastern slope we are now ascending. We pass Reno, the station nearest to Virginia City, and the celebrated Comstock Ledge, and run on to Truckee, where we learn that a snow shed over the track some miles west, has taken fire, and are detained and breakfast.

The Cornucopia of California has been poured over the Sierra Nevada. As we walk upon the platform of the station, after our repast, we notice fruit-stands and piles of choice melons, pears, peaches, plums and grapes of many varieties. Nearly all the passengers have clusters of White Muscats. While we pay our compliments to the breakfast, a member of the bar, who resides here, tells us that we must taste the Black Hamburgs, our choice green-house grapes, which ripen in the open air in California. He leaves us for a few minutes and returns with a large cluster of these grapes — such as the spies bore to the Hebrews from the Promised Land. Young Cecil admits that these equal the best he has seen in conservatories at home, and they find much favor with the ladies on their way westward.

In company with Mr. Hoadley, who, with his sons, runs a saw-mill on the Truckee, a stream, that brings from Lake Taho and the mountain a large supply of pine timber, I ride to his mill. Some of the logs which we see in the mill-pond, are five to six feet in diameter, and these are easily taken from the stream to the saw, by a sledge that runs under them and is drawn up by the water-wheel. The water-power and timber have built up here a flourishing village,—some thirty mills are planted on the falls of the Truckee, and one hundred and sixty millions of feet, or half the amount of lumber shipped from Bangor, are made here annually, giving at least one hundred thousand tons of freight and material to the railway. It is shipped hence as far as Elcho and White Pine, and for six dollars a thousand, or for five cents a ton per mile, over the Sierra to Sacramento.

Soon a telegram comes with instructions to advance and exchange passengers with the morning train from Sacramento. We slowly ascend the Sierra, on a gradient of 105 feet to the mile, with two engines, catching beautiful views through the ravines of mountains, with their diadems of snow and the sparkling Lake Downer far below us, encircled by tall pines. We wind around the lake as we ascend, we pass the summit and reach the scene of the fire, a few miles west of the summit, passing alternately through tunnels and snow sheds, all well constructed, the latter sustained by tall sticks of pine, ten to fifteen inches through, apparently hewn from the forest beside them, and leaving room for two tracks between them. On our way across the mountains, we pass through thirty miles of shed, divided by tunnels and open spaces into at least thirty-five sections.

The fire has run nearly two miles, from an open space to a tunnel, and the cinders are on the slope below us. Many of the ties, partially covered with earth, have been destroyed, and the rails are in some cases warped and twisted. Our passengers descend from the cars, each with a valise, shawl or some other appendage. Some stop to aid ladies across culverts. Some bear infants in their arms. As our procession advances the trunks and heavy articles are seized by Chinese trackmen, swung on long poles, and thus borne quietly along suspended from their shoulders. Can such strength spring from rice, or are they invigorated by a new diet? On the way we pass a like procession from the West, ascending, as we descend, the highest gradient of the Sierra Nevada, 116 feet to the mile. Soon we reach the western train, and ere long forget our efforts and fatigue in another set of silver palace cars which await our arrival. Again under weigh, we soon slowly descend the gradient and reach Sacramento, the second city of the State, 130 miles from San Francisco, with friends who have come in seven days from the Atlantic, and here we find comfortable quarters at the Golden Eagle.

Sacramento, California, Thursday, August 26th.

After a good night's sleep, and breakfast of melons, grapes, broiled salmon and English muffins, we meet a gentleman, originally from Boston, who offers to pilot us to the warehouses where grapes and pears are packed for transportation. Around this city, and on the rivers and railways between it and San Francisco, are some of the finest orchards, vineyards, and fruit gardens of California. The markets overflow with fruit, as the rivers do with salmon, and here the business of packing has begun, and the best mode of packing is still in debate, but the preference is given to small boxes, with slats on the sides, in crates or hampers, and some use sawdust or cork dust to sustain the grapes. Some fruit has been lost by delay or poor packing, but that which reaches Chicago and the eastern cities in six days or less, and is well packed, arrives in good condition and sells rapidly. A single carload of nine tons, which cost in California but $900, has paid a profit of $1,500 over freight and charges, and was then sold by retail at large profits.

We learn here that grapes are worth at the vineyards but one and one-half cents a pound for the wine-press, and new wine sells for twenty-five cents a gallon without the cask, and that grapes and pears command but two to five cents per pound for the best quality; that fruit gardens and vineyards yield nine thousand pounds of fruit to the acre, and that the market is overstocked with fruit. The vines and trees are yet young, and low as prices are, they bid fair to be lower with future growth, Chinese labor and competition.

A single township, which would not be missed in California, where individuals cultivate 30,000 acres, would suffice to give ninety thousand tons of fruit to the railway, or sixty carloads daily in six months; a supply of three carloads a day for each of our twenty larger Atlantic cities, where early and choice pears and plums and green-house grapes would be appreciated, could they be delivered at a cost of five cents per pound, and six cents per pound, freight and charges.

It is already apparent that the railways may send this freight through in six days with great profit, at six cents per pound, in express or emigrant trains, and there can be little doubt of a market when this is accomplished.

After visiting the markets, we present our letters of introduction to Governor Leland Stanford and Mr. Crocker, the President and Superintendent of the Central Pacific line, and congratulate them on the condition of their road, and learn from them that the income drawn from the line in May, June and July has been $1,637,007 in gold, or $2,182,676 in currency. This is nearly the same with the receipts of the Union Pacific line, for the same period, and shows that the two lines as a unit before their through freight is developed and with less than three trains on the average on the Union Pacific, are earning £37 a mile a week, or more than the great East Indian Railway earned last year, with many trains and a much higher cost per mile.*

Messrs. Stanford and Crocker gave us a cordial welcome. When I suggested the policy of carrying between sea and sea, in currency at $125 for first class, $75 for second class and $45 for emigrant passengers, they expressed a wish to go lower, and when I suggested as rates for through freight six cents a pound on perishable or valuable freight by express trains, five cents for first class and two and one-half cents for third class, or $1,200, $1,000 and $500 per carload, they expressed their readiness to accede. In the course of conversation they stated that, although their local charges were much below the rates by stage and wagon, they were well aware they were not the standard for prices across the continent; that with coal for fuel, at fair prices, and one lading and unlading for long distances, the cost of transit would be reduced.

It was obviously for their interest to take the freight and emigrants now carried across the Isthmus, and induce the owners of the steamers running to the Isthmus to transfer their steamers to the route between China and San Francisco. In reply to a suggestion from the Hon. Mr. Eldridge of Wisconsin, as to the interest on the national bonds issued in aid of the enterprise, Governor Stanford assured him the interest would be paid. While I conferred with the officials, Lord Cecil examined the shops and engines, and found the equipage

* See Appendix.

in good condition. He obtained here and from the vice-president a few days later, the following account of rolling stock, viz. :—

    166 locomotives received.
    24 shipped or in progress.
    148 passenger, express and baggage cars.
    2,174 freight cars.
    95 gravel cars.

We learn also that the new railway will be finished to Oakland or Alameda, within five miles by ferry, of San Francisco, by the 6th of September, as the tracklayers are completing it at the rate of fifteen miles a week, to be in season for the fair, from which the company expect to realize $40,000.

This railway will shorten the journey to the Atlantic at least ten hours. It passes through one of the best and most popular portions of California, abounding in fruit and grain. It has received from government a subsidy of two and one-half millions for one hundred and twenty-four miles; and as the governor states, has not thus far issued any mortgage bonds. There are no costly works upon the line; the highest gradient is fifty-three feet to the mile, and the governor hopes to send his fast trains through in four hours from the ferry in the harbor of San Francisco to Sacramento.

According to the best estimates I can form, the Union Pacific will be able to take, on the average, two hundred tons, and the Central Pacific one hundred and fifty tons of merchandise on their freight trains.

FRIDAY, August 27th.

As the line to Alameda is not yet open, we take the cars on another line to Vallejo. On our way, we pass through wheat fields and pastures; see many cattle and horses, and notice at each station many thousand sacks of wheat piled in the open air. The railway on which we travel is delivering eight thousand sacks of wheat daily on navigable waters.

In the cars a tall and portly gentleman addresses me by name, and reminds me of a summer twenty years since, which we passed together at Plymouth, when he, Dr. Merritt, was preparing to sail for California, as a young physician. He invites me to visit him at his country-seat at Oakland. He left with little property, but has prospered in California. He points out to us the forts and navy-yard, the Golden Gates and the rising city as we sail down the bay and meet the refreshing breezes of ocean, after a warm night at Sacramento, and by noon we land at San Francisco, as fresh as when we left Boston, without any feeling of fatigue, and learn that the gap caused by the fire has been closed behind us.

We take our quarters at the Lick House, a most comfortable inn, present our letters, and call on Messrs. Badger, Ralston, Mills and other gentlemen, and accept the invitation of Mr. Ralston to pass the 29th with him at his country seat, and to take a drive through the environs of San Francisco.

During the afternoon we visit, with Mr. Badger, the fruit market, where we find an abundance of choice vegetables, strawberries, and at least twenty varieties of delicious plums, pears, peaches and grapes of greenhouse varieties, but grown in the open air. We are invited to taste, and to buy at a few cents per pound. We visit the Exchange and Mercantile Library, well furnished with books, magazines and reading-rooms, and take from the shelf the Merchants' Magazine for December, 1856, in which I predict that the Pacific Railways would earn $9,000 a mile a year, or £36 a mile a week, which I am happy to find is already verified in the infancy of the enterprise.

SAN FRANCISCO, August 28th.

Here we receive welcome letters from home, dated ten days after our departure; and our young friend starts for the quicksilver mines of Almaden. At breakfast we meet Mr. Denman, the able superintendent of the public schools, who tells us that this city, with less than 140,000 people, has an average attendance of 15,000 pupils on its free schools, and expends on them half a million in gold yearly. We call on Mr. Stowe, of the Board of Trade, who tells me two-thirds of the people are urgent for a reduced tariff, and introduces me to many leading merchants, among them to Mr. Alfred Haraszthy, from Hungary, who devotes himself to the production and sale of wine.

I learn from him that most varieties of the grape thrive in California; that the produce per acre is fifty per cent. larger than in Europe; that the crop never fails; that new wine sells from the vineyard for a quarter of a dollar the gallon; that the cask costs eleven cents per gallon, and the wine is worth half a dollar the second year, when ready for bottling; but with the brandy, is sold by retail, when bottled, from $4.00 to $9.00 the dozen, and in some cases the sparkling wines are sold for $12.00 or $15.00 per dozen. Fair Port, and wine from the Burgundy grape, may be bought in the cask from sixty to seventy cents per gallon.

Considerable wine is sent to Germany to reinforce the poor wines of the Rhine. The vineyards on the foot hills have the preference for flavor.

Wine is fast becoming one of the great staples of California. The age of agriculture succeeds the age of gold, and the three W's,—Wheat, Wine and Woollens,—are in the ascendant, while the three F's,—Furs, Forests and Fisheries,—predominate in Alaska and British Columbia.

We call again on Mr. Ralston, the manager of the Bank of California, the chief banking institution of this city, and the advocate of specie, which exerts a great influence over the State. The banking house, a large and handsome stone building, stands on California Street, the Wall Street or State Street of the

Pacific, whose structures compare well with those in either of the streets of New York or Boston.

On a raised platform in a counting-room, which overlooks a large banking-room, sits Mr. Ralston, the cashier, and answers promptly yes or no, to the applications for money, and his reply is decisive.

Thirty-six clerks stand or write behind the counter of the bank, who draw on the average $175 a month in gold, and receive $50 or $75 as a compliment on the first of January.

Nearly all checks are paid and all deposits made in double eagles. Porters and clerks are constantly coming and going with bags of gold, and Chinese are counting and occasionally throwing out Mexican dollars. I have seen nothing like it for years in New York or Boston, and it is pleasant to see this young daughter of the Bay State setting so laudable an example to the mother and the sisters.

I listen to an anecdote of a firm in the dry goods trade, which, in 1862, purchased in New York, goods to the amount of $200,000, on a long credit, to be paid in currency. The goods rose, and the debtors sold at a large profit in gold, which rose also in value. The New York creditors, disturbed by the war, offered a discount of twenty-five per cent. for the money.

The $150,000 required was bought for $100,000 in gold, and the goods produced $300,000, and the proceeds invested in land, have since doubled.

Such have been the inducements to California to adhere to specie.

I am told by a lawyer that the Savings Banks of this city now have $16,000,000 on deposit, lent at ten to twelve per cent. on mortgage, and that most of the mechanics and most of the washerwomen are worth from $2,000 to $20,000.

At 4.40, P. M., Mr. Ralston calls with his carriage and takes us to the station. At Belmont we leave the cars for a light, tasteful omnibus that awaits us, and in five minutes, our party, which has grown to a dozen, are at the house of our host, a spacious mansion, at least fifty yards in depth and width, with rooms for fifty guests. Each of us is shown to a suite of rooms, chamber, dressing-room, bath-room and appendages.

At six we dine. In the evening a fire is lighted, as the night is cool, and we retire early, as we are to have a drive before breakfast.

BELMONT, August 29th.

We are called early to coffee, toast and eggs. At 7.30, A. M., we walk to the stables, which have stalls for more than forty horses, and there ten of us take seats in an open California carriage, with four horses. Our host, still in the prime of life, takes the reins, invites me to sit beside him, and away we go, across the country at the rate of ten to twelve miles per hour. We drive through wheat fields, beside hills covered with evergreen oaks, through the grounds of Mr. Hayward, who has recently sold his gold mine for $800,000, and pass through his stable of redwood, with a Gothic roof, whose rafters and beams are gilded.

Mr. Ralston stops in his garden to gather fresh plums and pears, and tells the gardener who assists him to say, that if Mr. H. does not appreciate them, we do.

After a drive through the pleasure grounds of Messrs. Parrot and Whipple, and ascending a fine eminence by a winding road, for a prospect, we return to breakfast. On our way, our host points out a tract of eleven hundred acres, bought by Mr. Burlingame, the Chinese Envoy, last year, for $55 the acre, which would now sell for $250.

We return to breakfast at 10, A. M., and in an hour we find our carriage, with fresh horses, again at the door. Lord Cecil has joined us, and again we are in rapid motion.

We visit the grounds of Mr. T. R. Selby, who invites us to examine his two acres of almond-trees, which resemble our largest peach-trees, and are now in full bearing. We pass a cactus, at least eight feet high, in the open air, and enter a garden devoted to grapes, fruit-trees and vegetables. In this enclosure of seven acres, says Mr. Selby, " the trees were out but six years, and last year gave us 1,400 bushels of fruit, most of which perished, as we could not use it, and the market was flooded."

Here were greenhouse grapes of many kinds, figs, walnuts, plums, peaches, pears and apples. Lawton blackberries, with luscious fruit, tall celery, gigantic cauliflower.

One gentleman comes to us with a fresh stripped fig, another with several kinds of plums, another with sprigs laden with blackberries, others with pears and peaches—all insist that we must eat. We are in the Garden of Eden, and tempted as Eve never could have been, by our warm-hearted friends.

We would have had the scene photographed, to exhibit the fruits and hospitality of California.

As I would not venture to eat much fruit, Mr. Selby says he will send me a box to take home with me, a promise he fully redeemed. At his house I meet some of the fair ladies of the country.

On the grounds of Mr. Atherton one of our party measures the smooth and thrifty bough of an apple-tree, one inch and an eighth in thickness, which has ninety-nine apples on a length of three feet, and several feet of new wood at its extremity.

And here I recognize the virtues of alkali, for I am told the sage bush has grown and alkali been traced in California. The bark of the apple-tree shows the power of soda and potash.

We enter the grounds of the Messrs. Barons, late owners of the quicksilver mines at Almaden, an English family, which left England for religious freedom, and has realized wealth by mining. Here a rill has been led from the foot hills, through pipes, and in the dry season an English lawn, of intense green, is before us.

Evergreen oaks and Australian firs throw their shade over a trout pond. Dahlias are luxuriant, and vistas open for fine prospects across beautiful pleasure-grounds.

After an excursion which occupies five hours so pleasantly, we leave our host behind, and return at 4, P. M., to dress for dinner, and meet him at 6, P. M., at the table, with several new guests, some of whom are senators and members of Congress.

At 7, P. M., he returns with us to San Francisco, and lands us safely at our hotel.

August 30th.

Mr. Alvord kindly takes us out this morn for a drive along the south-eastern side of the harbor; points out the dry-dock, scooped from the rock, where two vessels can be repaired at once, and shows us the first rolling-mill of the Pacific, where old rails and scrap iron are renovated. Its capacity is now limited, but the site is excellent and the works may be expanded, and will be very useful. Thence we drive rapidly through new streets, and beside the tall lupins and other wild flowers, so well pictured by Fremont, to the cliffs, near the Golden Gates, a favorite resort of the citizens. Here California has preserved some of the gifts of nature—a great number of seals and sea-lions, which are seen disporting in their native element, climbing the rocks and shaking the spray from their sides, upon the sea-weed.

You pass through the Cliff House to a long piazza in the rear, and within twenty rods you see large rocks, like those of Nahant, rising from the sea, and seals and sea-lions rolling and gambolling upon them without fear or disturbance, to the great amusement of both young and old. Compared with this, our deer park hides its diminished head and loses its attractions.

Returning from the cliff, we ride with Mr. Denman to the Lincoln Grammar School, before which stands a statue of Lincoln. It is a large structure, with 22 rooms and a hall, together accommodating 1,250 pupils with separate seats.

The assistants are ladies, whose salaries are from $800 to $900, and the reading, responses, writing and drawing of the boys do credit to their teachers—the boys look healthful, and the percentage of absentees is less than five per cent. Thence to the Denman School, for eight hundred girls, with fourteen rooms, and here we are struck with the reading, writing and map-drawing.

Lieutenant-Commander Blake has gone to the navy-yard, but my young friend, Lord Cecil, and I are called upon for brief addresses, and the young ladies sing to the piano. Mr. Denman tells us that half of them have pianos at home.

A part of the morning still remains, and I accompany a gentleman to a woollen mill, near the forts and opposite to the Isle of Alcantraz, passing high bluffs on the way, already fast yielding to the advance of population. My wish is to see the Chinese at their toils. Here a capital of $450,000 has been planted in substantial brick buildings, and makes fair returns; and here one hundred skilled artisans and one hundred and fifty Chinese are assembled, and when trade is active these numbers are nearly doubled.

The company make very soft and white blankets, affghans and robes for sleighs and open carriages, flannels of various patterns, colors and figures, and woollen skirts. The dyeing and other difficult work falls to the skilled artisans, who receive $3, while the Chinese draw but $1 per day, in gold, and do the weaving, spinning, sewing and rough work of the factory. The wool comes from the sheep of California, and is bought for twenty-one cents a pound. It is in part half-blood Merino, in part Leicestershire and Southdown.

The foreman of the factory is from Massachusetts, where he was trained in factories at Andover and Salisbury. In our walk he points out to me tin cases of peanut oil from China, which costs eighty-five cents a gallon, and is considered preferable to lard or mineral oil. In its taste it resembles salad oil. If Marseilles can convert the peanuts of Africa, and Providence the cotton-seed of the South into olives by their alchemy, and both peanuts and cotton-seed abound here, while olives grow at Los Angelos, why may we not throw off our dependence for sweet oil on France and Italy?

I learn that last year California produced twelve millions and this year will yield fourteen million pounds of wool. The ewes drop their lambs in February, and are sheared early in the season.

In the autumn the sheep are sheared again and the lambs are sheared also, as a preventive against scab. The average yield is from four to five pounds.

The foreman speaks of his acquaintance, Colonel Hollister, who in 1852 crossed the mountains with twelve hundred sheep, losing a third of them before he reached the coast. He purchased ranches, and his sheep increased and now number sixty-four thousand, in thirty-two flocks, each under the care of a shepherd.

His sales of wool, wethers and lambs are said to reach $100,000 yearly, and his flocks still increase. As land rises, he sells his ranches for wheat and vineyards, and buys others further south. He is now one of the millionaires of the country.

In the evening I visit my friend, Mr. Joseph Perry, Jr., formerly well known in State Street, Boston, who now lives pleasantly in San Francisco.

In the course of the day, I meet Mr. Glidden, of the Boston firm of Glidden & Williams, who arrived yesterday in seven days from Boston, and assures me that he felt more vigorous on his arrival, than when he left home.

In the course of the evening, I meet Mr. Fay, a cousin of Colonel Fay of Chelsea, near Boston, who brings me some specimens of a second crop of barley, raised by irrigation, a few miles from the city. His friend, a gentleman from Chili, after taking a crop of sixty bushels of this grain from an acre, conceived the idea of irrigating the land as they did in Chili.

The water was let on early in August, and the crop reaped in October; the yield was 6,200 pounds of grain, or more than a hundred and ten bushels. Where, I ask, are the limits of the fertility of this strange country, already one of the chief granaries of the world?

We hear of our defeat in the boat-race, but in our race with England for this fine country a few years since, we were more successful. We won a prize that is becoming daily more valuable.

In the evening I call on a noted chemist, who had analyzed the alkali of the plains a few years since, and found the residuum like that of sea-water, chiefly chloride of sodium, soda, potash, lime and magnesia.

TUESDAY, August 31st.

My companions, who are soon to cross the ocean, are impatient to return, and Lord Cecil leaves this morn for the mines of Grass Valley and the famous Comstock Ledge, proposing to meet Mr. Blake at Virginia City, and to join me on Friday at Reno, on the Central Pacific.

With Mr. Blake I visit the office and works of the San Francisco Assay and Refining Company, where gold and silver from the mines are reduced to bars and stamped for exportation.

The capacity of these works, owned chiefly by the Bank of California, is sufficient to refine a quarter of a million in gold, and one-tenth of that amount of silver, daily, and their assay and stamps are respected both in Asia and Europe. They rival the mint in the extent of their operations, and their skilled artisans earn eight dollars a day.

We trace gold and silver ores, through crucibles, acids and baths to the solid ingots, which are cast in our presence, and near the works observe a marsh, converted by Chinese irrigation into a verdant garden.

We confer with Mr. Cohen, a gentleman conversant with land, to whom we are referred by Mr. Ralston, as to the value of the land granted by Congress to the Central Pacific line. He informs us that a part is covered with timber of growing value, a part fit for cultivation, a part for pasturage, and much of it is in alkali plains. Without water he rates the value at half a dollar per acre, but triples it if water shall be found accessible, and thinks it may possibly command a higher price, as land has taken many sudden flights in value in this country. Mr. Cohen gives us the distance by the new Western Pacific Railway from Sacramento to the ferries of Oakland and Alameda at one hundred and twenty-four miles, and the more circuitous route by San Jose as forty-six miles longer. He informs us that the Western Pacific is pledged for $2,500,000 to government, but has issued no mortgage bonds and is held principally by Messrs. Stanford, Huntington, Hopkins and Crockers, who control the Central Pacific Railway also.

During an interview with Captain Eldridge, the agent of the mail steamers to China, I learn that the last steamship brought seventy-five cabin passengers at $250, and seven hundred Chinese, with considerable tea at $15 per measurement ton.

The line from New York *via* Panama brings usually five hundred emigrants, a few cabin passengers and full freights, by each steamer; the rate for goods not charged by the foot is reduced to a cent and a half a pound in gold, equivalent, with insurance, interest and other charges, to two and a half cents in currency, by the railway.

I devote some hours to calls on eminent physicians, to ascertain the prospects for a young kinsman, and have a pleasant talk with Senator Stewart of Nevada.

WEDNESDAY, September 1st.

My agreeable companion, Lieutenant-Commander Blake, leaves this morn for Virginia City, and I confer with Mr. Gray, the consulting engineer of the Central Pacific Railway, who tells me that his line must go to Ogden, either by the track of the Union or by its own track, which in his opinion could be completed for less than three millions. He gives me many facts relating to the line, and satisfies me that Promontory is no place for a connection.

In the course of the day, I call on Mr. J. P. Raymond, a flour merchant, to whom I have letters of introduction, and stop on the way to admire bags of very large potatoes and onions, whose price is but seventy-five cents per cental.

Mr. Raymond shows me some Santa Clara flour, very white and fine, which he thinks equal to Plant's brand of St. Louis flour, and might sometimes be sent to Boston at the rate of two and a half cents a pound.

Wheat can be raised with profit in California at $1.25 per cental. With wheat at this rate and flour at a corresponding rate of $4.50 a barrel, California flour could be sold in China for the price of rice, and the consumption would absorb the whole surplus of the coast.

Ships taking flour to Shanghai or Japan at sixty cents per barrel, might return with sugar or with tea at five or six dollars per measurement ton, and vessels taking coal to China and Japan might take rice, tea or sugar to San Francisco, and then load with wheat at ninety cents the cental for Europe.

I learn that business is for the moment depressed in California, that the earthquake checked building, and led some Eastern capitalists to withdraw their funds, which are now beginning to return, and this has led to a call on the Secretary of the Treasury for a transfer of credits from New York to San Francisco.

The city suffers from a trade-union of the housewrights, who require $4.00 in gold for eight hours' work, which the builders decline to pay. With wages at $2.25 in currency in Chicago for ten hours' work, they cannot long continue at the present rates in San Francisco.

I learn from Mr. Glidden that the Chinese are going into the copper mines, which will not pay at the rate of American labor, and that Flint and Peabody are, with Chinese labor, converting yearly 7,000 bales of Manilla grass into cordage.

I pass the evening in pleasant conversation with Senator Stewart and Governor Stanford, discussing the prospects of the Central Pacific line.

I inquire as to the Beckwith pass, across the Sierra Nevada, which lies fourteen hundred feet below the present summit of the line. They tell me it has been surveyed and found impracticable, from interlocking cliffs, deep ravines and frequent freshets of the Feather River, beside which it would have led to a circuit of a hundred miles to reach the Truckee River, and to a run of forty miles through the snow region. The governor states also, that the snow-sheds have generally cost seventeen thousand dollars a mile, and for a few miles, some designed to shield the line from avalanches, have cost seventy thousand dollars a mile.

These gentlemen give me an account of the wheat culture in California. In one district the wheat fields are continuous for fifty miles. One man, a Mr. M., came here four years since, with five thousand dollars. Converting it into paper, he bought college land scrip, (possibly that of Massachusetts,) at seventy-five cents, and sowed wheat on the land purchased.

With one team of six horses, with a gang-plough, he could take care of five hundred acres, and he went boldly into cultivation. He now has one hundred and thirty thousand acres, seventeen thousand of them in wheat, and will have thirty thousand in wheat next year, and holds his land at twenty dollars or more an acre.

Thus are sudden fortunes made here, and I hear from others,

of not less than twenty capitalists who have retired from trade, whose fortunes are rated from one to three millions each.

The course of trade is changing. Money has been dear, and the receipts of goods irregular; large fortunes have been made by men who have watched the markets, and as stocks were reduced, bought up the residue to make cent. per cent. profits. The railways will bring regular supplies and more steady prices.

We may well anticipate that merchants will come here with capital; that warehouses will be built at Oakland and Alameda, to store tea, coffee, sugar, rice and wool, near the tracks, and large importations be made and held for inland consumption. That the merchants of Chicago, St. Paul and St. Louis will watch the course of prices, and as they fluctuate buy on the Atlantic or Pacific, sending their orders by telegraph.

THURSDAY, September 2d.

This morn Governor Stanford tells me that the Central freight engines will take ten loaded freight cars over the summit, and then run with twenty cars, and I was confirmed on my conclusion, that the Central line may average fifteen and the Union Pacific twenty cars or more in their daily routine of duty.

Desirous to see Oakland, the future terminus of the Pacific lines, and to pay my promised visit to Dr. Merritt, I take the ferry-boat this morn and run across the harbor. A train of cars awaits us at the end of a long pier, four miles from the city, and we soon reach a large tract of land rising gradually from a plain to a gentle eminence, admirably adapted for gardens or a commercial city.

The train stops every mile, and three miles from the landing I take a coach, which soon carries me to the seat of my friend, and here on the height of land, I find forty acres of pleasure grounds, studded with fruit-trees and vines and ornamental pines and firs, to which Europe and Australia have contributed, and along a street bordering on the enclosure, six or eight fine residences, which my friend has erected.

I am kindly received and shown the prospect from the cupola, a fine view across pleasure grounds, to a portion of the harbor, which resembles a lake walled in from the sea, and have a charming view of the peninsula.

This property, under the influence of the railway, is progressing in value, and I learn from a third party that three hundred thousand dollars has been offered for the homestead.

And now I must bid adieu to the Pacific, to this land of fruit and breadstuffs, now bound to the Atlantic States by indissoluble bonds of iron, by rail and telegraph. If I were a young man I should be tempted to cast anchorage and identify my fortunes with California.

Returning to the Lick House, I dine with Professor Horsford and his fair daughter, and at four o'clock, P. M., embark in the good steamer Yosemite for Sacramento, where I am to take the cars next morn at six o'clock on the Central Pacific.

A week later and the Western Pacific, on which the company is fast laying the rails, would have reduced my passage from fourteen hours to four, and save me nearly half a day on the journey; but I find good company and a pleasant state-room, and a box of fruit from Mr. Selby, the newly elected mayor, awaits me at the steamer landing, and is safely placed in my state-room. During the evening a fruit-dealer tells me that he is going East to visit his parents and arrange for the shipment of fruit; that he proposes to pack his choice grapes in sawdust, and thinks they can be placed in the cars at six cents and delivered in Eastern cities at twelve or thirteen cents per pound.

SACRAMENTO, Friday, September 3d.

After a good night's rest in my state-room, I secure berths and seats for myself and friends in a silver palace car to Promontory for five dollars each, and at six, A. M., start for home, with some seventy passengers.

For twenty-six miles we pass by vineyards and wheat fields, and then begin the ascent of the foot hills, then of the Sierra, and in eighty miles we rise with ruling gradients of eighty-six to one hundred and sixteen feet per mile to the summit, with snow-clad hills around us. We catch many charming views down deep ravines, and then descend by Lake Downer, which we see a thousand feet below us, to the Truckee Valley. On our way we pass through some fifteen short tunnels, over eight bridges, chiefly of substantial trestle work, across ravines and through some thirty-five sections of snow-sheds, separated by tunnels, bridges or openings.

Great pains have been taken to avoid detention by snow or avalanches in the spring or winter.

At Reno, Lord Cecil and Lieut. Commander Blake join me. I learn from them that the mines of Grass Valley do well under improved processes for extraction, and that at the Comstock Ledge the yield of the year will probably reach nine millions.

SATURDAY, September 4th.

Among our companions is an intelligent trader from White Pine, who has been to purchase stores; he assures me that the silver ore is rich, and in his opinion continuous in many mines, although some of it is found in large chimneys. He also states that stamp mills, and aqueducts from the mountains, are in progress, and that there is little doubt the yield of silver will, by January, rise to half a million per month.

We breakfast at Elcho, the future capital of Nevada, where we see several fine stages, each with six horses, ready to start for White Pine. Our seventy passengers, by accessions at Reno and Elcho, have now grown to a hundred.

The road is in fine order, if we except thirty-five miles beyond Elcho, which will require more ballast before winter, and it will be well to imbed the tracks over the Sierra more deeply in the gravel, as some ties were destroyed by the burning snow-sheds. We examine the line from the rear platfrom on sections previously passed in the night, and notice, that with three exceptions, the station-houses and engine-houses of the Central Pacific are of wood. The buildings of the Union Pacific are of brick or stone. We find the track and road-bed in excellent condition.

We reach Promontory at 11 o'clock P. M., before the Eastern train, which is a few hours late, and start two hours late for the East. The state of things at this point and the waste of two hours' time by each train, the confusion that attends the interchange in the open air, with no building near us, except those under canvass, which are fortunately in a dry climate, shows the importance of an early adjustment of all questions between the companies and the erection of a proper station at Ogden.

SUNDAY, September 5th.

We start again in our new train with berths in Pullman cars at 2, A. M., and after breakfast take our places again with several engineers on the rear platform. Here the new road obviously requires surfacing and widening. The track, it is true, is smooth and safe for the present, but the earth from the embankment has been thrown up for ballast. Rain here is rare, and the material of fair quality, but some surfacing remains to be done, which can be now done more cheaply than when the track was laid. Several steam shovels are by the roadside. Mormons are ready with their teams to take up materials from the sides at twenty cents per yard; a great reduction from the contract prices, and gravel trains may now be employed to advantage in surfacing.

As we cross Green River, we notice an extensive basin encircled by mountains, with a narrow outlet, and here it would seem that a dam may at some future day form a great water-power, and flow back the water or raise it by pumps for irrigation.

MONDAY, September 6th.

We again pass the Laramie Plains and breakfast at the Laramie hotel, and meet our friend, Dr. Latham, who accompanies us to Cheyenne, and as we ascend the summit, points out Pike's Peak, Mount Agassiz and other snow-clad mountains and the perpetual snow-line, five thousand feet above us.

At Sherman the pastures are green, and we see three bands of antelopes near the summit. Again we are struck with the skilful engineering by which the line has been piloted through ravines, and along the mountain side without tunnels or heavy cuts in rock or high embankments.

At Cheyenne we meet a band of music, on a staging erected in a huge wagon. Here is a county meeting to congratulate a newly-elected officer, and here our train receives a considerable accession from Denver. We number at least one hundred and twenty passengers, and launch again upon the plains. From the Sherman summit for at least one hundred miles, I am struck with the superior quality of the gravel, disintegrated granite, fit for a gravel walk, admirably suited for the surface of the road. If gravel is not found further east, the track might be raised a foot by sand from the plains, and a coating of but four inches of gravel over the sand would make an excellent ballast. Seven hundred tons of gravel could be sent out on a train over descending grades, and one train would give surface to half a mile of railway, and three or four gravel trains could do the work in a twelvemonth.

As we pass over the plains I fall into conversation with Mr. Edwards, a very intelligent merchant, who is now but ten days from Vancouver's Island. He is a native of England, but has married in the United States. He tells me the Province has suffered from the decay of commerce since the Treaty of Reciprocity was repealed; that it has great resources in its timber, and seeks for commerce with the Union; that in that Province two fifteen-pound salmon can be bought for a bit, or twelve and a half cents, and fine halibut of thirty to one hundred and fifty pounds, at one cent a pound; that the sea, when he left, was almost alive with candle fish and herring, and one boat from the shore had harpooned eleven whales. On our Atlantic front the salmon and halibut are two to four days on their way from the fishing grounds, in vessels packed with ice, to Boston.

Thence they are distributed, summer and winter, through the great cities of the Atlantic States. A propeller could, in three days, run down from Vancouver's Island to the terminus of the Central Pacific, at Oakland, and deliver her fish in ice, not at Boston prices, viz., twelve or fifteen cents per pound for halibut, and thirty to fifty cents for salmon, but at three cents per pound for each of them, and in four days more these fish could be distributed through the valley of the Missouri and Mississippi, and in winter the frozen and smoked fish could be distributed through the country.

On the Atlantic front, nearly two hundred thousand tons of fresh, dry, smoked and pickled fish are annually landed for consumption. Why may not half that quantity be landed on our Pacific shores, from more prolific fisheries, and three-fourths of that amount be sent eastward by the Pacific Railways?

We meet, also, Mr. Jacobs, a stage proprietor from Colorado, who tells us that the branch from Denver to Cheyenne, for half its length, viz., to Evans, will be finished this year, and the residue next year, and I subsequently learn from the Secretary of the Board of Trade of Denver that forty thousand cattle will be killed and shipped during the fall and winter from Colorado to Omaha, on their way to Chicago, and bring $240 a carload to the Union Pacific Railway. This must add at least $400,000 to the revenue of the Union Pacific line, and will be a new accession to the trade of Chicago.*

TUESDAY, September 7th.

We breakfast at Grand Isle, an important station, notice good grass on the plains, and luxuriant meadows below Kearney. At Columbus we pass the proposed terminus of a branch from Sioux City on the extension of the line from Duluth on Lake Superior, through St. Paul and Mankato to Sioux City. This branch will bring Columbus, on the Union Pacific, ninety-two miles west of Omaha, within five hundred miles of the navigable waters of Lake Superior, and within three hundred and fifty miles of the great lumber mart and saw-mills of St. Paul, and the Falls of St. Anthony. Lumber worth ten dollars at St. Paul may be delivered at Columbus at less than twenty dollars per thousand, almost as cheap as at Chicago. The iron of Lake Superior may be sent with it, and return loads of wheat, cattle, fruit, fish and minerals from Colorado may be sent back to Lake Superior. This connection must give great advantages to the Union Pacific, in any rivalry with the Kansas Pacific, and enable it to supply that line with lumber.

Mr. Jacobs states that large droves of cattle are driven to Colorado from Texas, where steers are sold for eight or ten dollars each. These are fattened on the plains and then driven across the mountains to California, and this is subsequently confirmed by a gentleman from California, who states that prior to 1864, Spanish cattle were sold in California for the value of their hides and tallow, that the rains failed so that drought destroyed a large portion of their stock, and that steers worth five cents east of the mountains now sell for nine cents a pound, on the hoof, in California.

It is obvious to me that a cattle train might be run from

* See Appendix.

Cheyenne to Sacramento, or even down to Oakland for $400 or $500 per car, with benefit to both the railways. We make up an hour of our lost time, pass a branch to the Missouri at Fremont, and reach Omaha at 2, P. M.,—in less than five days from the Pacific.

Desirous to send home specimens of Mr. Selby's fruit, I take my box to the office of the United States Express Company, pay their price of ten cents per pound, and beg them to deliver it as soon as it arrives,—as it may in seven days from the Pacific, and to mark fruit upon it; but all my care is unavailing. This dilatory express company takes six days for its delivery, and on the eleventh day from San Francisco most of the plums and pears have perished. Enough, however, survive this neglect to convince my friends that fruit may be sent in six days from California to Boston.

At Omaha we meet an assemblage of railway men; the vice-president and superintendent of the Central Pacific, the officials of the Union Pacific, Messrs. Morris of Philadelphia, and the Messrs. Pullman of Chicago. Mr. Ames, the president of the Union Pacific, is also expected.

And here I learn that the Union Pacific has on its line, sixty thousand cords of wood, contracted for before the coal mines were opened, and costing about ten dollars a cord, and now to be superseded by cheap and excellent coal. The substitution of the latter must reduce two-thirds the cost of fuel. Much of this wood may be sold or used for kindling, but it would do the line injustice if we should carry the extra cost of this wood into our estimate of the cost of transportation. It was purchased on a large scale to expedite the enterprise, under a former administration.

WEDNESDAY, September 8th.

This morning I have a conference with the officials of the two lines, as to the rates of freight and fare, and the policy of running faster trains, both of freight and passengers.

The time from the Pacific to Omaha will at once be reduced twelve hours, by the completion of the Western Pacific. A fast train, with emigrant cars attached, will, by October, run through weekly, in less than six days between New York and San Francisco; but it is deemed wise for the residue of the year, to allow six and a half days, for the regular passenger trains, while the road is green, so that in case of detention they may have it in their power to make up time, and preserve their connections.

It is proposed, also, to put on fast freight trains, for fruit and express matter, and send with them the second-class passengers and emigrants. Although there are unsettled questions between the two lines, the superintendents appear to act in perfect harmony. Unity of action and good-fellowship will be most conducive to the success of these enterprises. Each day saved will increase the travel, for each day gained will save the passenger in time, meals and lodgings, at least twelve dollars.

In the afternoon my companions leave me for Chicago, where I hope to join them; they thus gain time for young Cecil to visit the machine shops at Hannibal and Aurora. I remain a day to confer with Mr. Ames, and towards evening walk with Mr. Parker, of Omaha, to the top of the bluffs above the city. Here we find the first State House or Capitol of Nebraska, now resigned to the city for a college. It stands in a commanding position, overlooks the whole city, the opposite heights of Council Bluffs, and the valley of the Missouri. The city is beneath us on two terraces, with streets a hundred feet wide, crossing each other, some of which ascend the bluffs. It is already nearly two miles long by half a mile in width, and new houses are in progress.

A grove of fine young trees stands behind the college. We enter the grounds of Dr. Lowe, an old resident, and find his house embowered in trees, and his garden full of grapes, plums, pears and peaches, a little later in their ripening than those of California, for we are here a thousand feet above the sea.

During the evening, having made objections to the weight of the Pullman cars, I am invited by Mr. Pullman to hear his views on the subject.

He urges that safety in case of collisions is secured by strong and substantial cars; that the weight is divided upon twelve wheels, under two tracks or bogies; that the length, closets and bedding insure space and comfort, but necessarily increase weight; and that the cars are popular, run full, and the public cheerfully pay for safety and comfort; and if the trains do not run as fast as some in Europe, the passengers need not stop for meals or lodging; that in all cases, the railway companies hold half the stock in his cars and divide the profits, which average seventeen per cent.

The weight of a train of four Pullmans, a baggage car and a dining car, without passengers, is not far from a hundred and fifty tons, without engine and tender. Should we ever apply the power now used, to a light English express train, we may possibly accomplish the journey from sea to sea, in three and a half days, or at the rate between London and Liverpool, and then balance despatch against comfort. It may be that comfort will turn the scale in favor of Pullman.

He is very popular with the ladies. At present the cost of a passage from Boston to the Pacific is $153 in paper, equivalent to $112 in gold, and the extra cost of berths and meals is equivalent to about five dollars per day in gold.

THURSDAY, September 9th.

The train of the Chicago and Northwestern, by which Mr. Ames is expected, is behind time, and I accompany Mr. Nichols across the river, to confer with General Dodge, the able and experienced engineer of the company. It is indebted to him and his corps of officers, for its excellent route through a wilderness.

We pass the "bottoms" where the wild sunflower stands nine feet high, giving proof of the strength of the soil. We gather its seeds as we sit in our open carriage. We rise gradually thirty feet above the river bank to Council Bluffs, where the ascent still continues.

General Dodge occupies a modest, vine-covered cottage, and still suffers from a wound received in the war. His heart is in the Union Pacific, and he has evinced his confidence by large investments in its stock and bonds.

He thinks a branch of 853 miles should be made from Granger, 877 miles west of Omaha, to Portland, in Oregon. This would fall into the valley of the Snake River and open a route to Montana, and bring the chief seaport of Oregon within 2,218 miles of Chicago.

I find it would also bring it within 2,140 miles of Lake Superior, *via* Columbus and Sioux City.

General Dodge has found a line through the Beckworth pass which he thinks may eventually be opened.

At the present moment the Californians are busy making a line to Oregon, in or near the valley of the Sacramento, and another up the valley of the St. Joachim. These will open a fertile and populous country, and inure to the benefit of both companies.

The possibility of effecting the other improvements and of making other lines across the mountains, may best be used to effect a union of the Union and Central lines under one organization, a measure which would benefit the country and add to the strength and efficiency of both enterprises.

General Dodge estimates the amount due from the Central line and from government, and the surplus property of the Union Pacific at the close of August, as not far from eight millions. From this the cost of completion and floating debt are to be deducted.

He thinks the Union Pacific has some advantages over the Central line. Easier grade, bolder curves, abundance of coal, no undulations in its gradients, a long and easy descent across the plains, and less snow in winter.

On the other side I should place more ballast, more timber, more fruit, fish and local business on the Central. Each line has its good qualities and advantages and may well enter into close alliance with the other.

As Mr. Ames has not arrived and I have nearly accomplished my mission, I conclude to take the cars for Chicago, *via* St. Joseph and the Chicago, Burlington and Quincy Railway. The route is longer than that by the Chicago and Northwestern, but the rates are the same, and after a hearty dinner I again cross the river and take the cars at 4, P. M., with some sixty passengers bound for St. Joseph, Chicago, Louisville and St. Louis.

With a young gentleman from New York, I succeed in obtaining the last section and two last berths in the sleeping car, for which we pay the reduced rate of a dollar and a half each.

Our route is along the intervales of the river, rich bottom lands in high grass or corn. The line has been made at small expense by throwing up the soil and leaving a ditch on either side, often filled with water from recent rains. At some points it has been overflowed and settled and a strong force is bringing it up to grade. It requires gravel and increased width of road-bed, otherwise the track will soon be injured and speed diminished.

A farmer, at least six feet two inches high, whose ruddy face and well rounded form show that fortune has smiled on him, sits near me. After an absence of twenty years from Kentucky, he is returning with his wife and child from Monterey, California, to visit his kindred.

He tells me that he thought many did not take land enough to enable them to live comfortably, but that he had taken two thousand acres, for a stock farm, which cost him five dollars an acre; that he fenced it with red wood, which stood well after it had been down for thirteen years; that his land was now worth fifty dollars an acre.

That from June to October, cows required some green food to keep them in milk, and this may account for the fact that California still draws from the East its cheese and butter.

His neighbors plough six acres a day with a team of six horses and sower and harrow attached to a gang-plough with three shares, and thus one man ploughs, sows and covers his grain.

When he has sown his seed he engages aid, either changing work or hiring men, and puts on a header and three wagons, and cuts thirty acres of wheat per day, and stacks the heads in the field, and then engages a portable mill to thresh and sack the grain at ten or fifteen cents a bushel, and thus one man may cultivate three hundred to five hundred acres and gather ten or fifteen thousand bushels, and take a crop of volunteer grain in the succeeding year.

He adds that sheep worth but $1.50 in Colorado are worth $3.50 at Monterey, and are often driven across the mountains. Here also is freight for the railways.

A German from Sonoma, California, distributes his grapes among the ladies, and invites us to taste his Sonoma wine from the Burgundy grape.

He informs us that the current price of good light wine in Sonoma, the second year, is forty to sixty cents per gallon, and the vineyards are rapidly improving.

FRIDAY, September 10th.

As our train is a little behind time, we are called to an early breakfast, on the Hannibal and St. Joseph line.

Finding "quail" upon the card, I call for quail, but the quail of this country does not fly, but swim, and it comes to me with fins in place of wings, but deserves commendation.

We are now crossing a fertile section of Missouri, on the Hannibal and St. Joseph line, and find a good track and fine farms in grass and corn, and many brick and painted houses, often with groves around them. The corn, however, has suffered from a wet season. The road is in good condition, but ballasted with stone as large as eggs. We pass many orchards, cross the Mississippi by a noble bridge of stone and iron, and enter Quincy, a city of thirty-six thousand people, at $10\frac{3}{4}$ o'clock in the morning.

And here we find there is a break in the connection, and we have seven hours at our disposal, which I devote to my journal, to a walk through the city, and a visit to the machine-shops.

The city is built on ground rising from the river. At the landing I find several steamers; on the eminence a parade-ground and wide avenues with brick and stone stores and a large hotel, where at the early hour of $12\frac{1}{2}$, P. M., I find an excellent dinner,—soup, several kinds of meat, a variety of vegetables, fruit, jelly, pastry and ice-cream.

The city does credit to the distinguished family in Massachusetts from which it derives its name, and is now nearly as large as Boston was when the elder Quincy begun the Quincy market, the first step in its progress from a provincial town to a flourishing city.

The foreman of the machine-shop walks with me through the shops, points out his engines, draws attention to his steel tires, some from Krupp's Prussian Works, thinks they will run 500,000 miles, and reduce cost of running.

He has recently been over the whole of the Union Pacific, on a visit to officers transferred from the Chicago, Quincy and Burlington line. He has examined the coal, thinks the line will soon be run at less cost per mile *than any line in the Western States*, on account of the superiority of its coal, road-bed and climate.

At Evanston, a mile and a half from the track, he found a

vein of coal thirty feet thick, of good quality, with a track graded to it. He has been over the line on an engine, and considers it in its curves, gradients, coal and road-bed, the best line he has ever seen.

Thinks the company has been a little extravagant in building much of it through the hills on embankments, and considers it in some respects superior to the C. Q. and B. line.

I have soon a proof of the excellence of the latter line. At 6.40, P. M., I enter the sleeping-car, and in twelve hours am landed at the station of the Illinois Central line in Chicago, after a pleasant run of two hundred and eighty-five miles. In the evening I watch from the rear platform the track, which is well ballasted and in good condition, and sleep pleasantly from 9, P. M., until we enter the Illinois Central line, near Chicago, and here, such is the pressure of traffic, we are obliged, as at Montreal, to alight outside of the station, ample as are its dimensions.

Twenty years since, when this station was in progress, I was a witness on the trial of a case as to the injury done to an estate by severance from its water-front by this station. The owner claimed large damages for injury, and I ventured to predict benefit in place of injury. The land he professed to think was ruined, is now worth $1,800 per foot of frontage, and occupied by a hotel.

SATURDAY, September 11th.

At the Sherman House this morn, I find Lieut. Commander Blake, and after breakfast take with him the cars of the Michigan Central for Niagara Falls.

Having criticized the Pacific lines, I am led to examine again the road-bed of this excellent railway. I find its ties imbedded to the surface, but the width of its road rarely more than ten feet. And yet its track stands well. It sends its cars through with speed and promptitude; has thirty-six trains daily on its single track, and has for twenty years never killed a passenger. We travel here with an intelligent dealer in live stock, from Council Bluffs, who thinks a cattle train across the mountains from the valley of the Platte would command a large number of cattle and horses at $500 per carload. We meet, also, Mr. B., a very intelligent gentleman from Chicago, who tells me that the farmers of the Mississippi Valley find sheep unprofitable, and are replacing them with cattle.

How can it be otherwise, when we place a higher duty on wool than we do on woollens, and compel the sheep-owners of the La Plata to sell their wool to England for five pence a pound.

Is there not danger that we shall make them dairy farmers, when we compel them to sacrifice the pelts of their sheep to pay the cost of boiling them down for tallow?

SUNDAY, September 12th.

We breakfast, cross the river to the Clifton House, by the Suspension Bridge, and rejoin our young English friend. We then attend church at Drummondsville, and enjoy the magnificent spectacle of the waterfall. Its thunders are still heard, and its rushing waters are still viewed from the forests which line the banks of the cataract.

MONDAY, September 13th.

Lord Cecil leaves us for Montreal, and after an early breakfast, we take seats at 7, A. M., for Albany and Boston on a car of the New York Central line, the fast train having passed during the night. From Niagara to Rochester I inspect the track from the rear platform.

The country through which we pass has a rich but moist soil, better adapted for agriculture than for railways, and the ballast, as the conductor tells me, has in some places been drawn seventy-five miles. The surface has been raised by successive layers of earth and gravel. A gentleman tells me he has seen the road when trains could run on it but ten miles an hour; they can now make forty, for the ties are well bedded and secured. They are, however, a foot shorter than on the Pacific lines, and the road-bed slopes from a point about one foot beyond the ends of the ties, towards the ditch. In the centre of the track the ballast is level with the surface of the tie, and then declines towards the end of the tie for drainage.

Below Rochester, the road-bed widens at the surface to about twelve feet—measuring as I do, by the eye. It will be very easy to keep the Pacific lines in as good a condition as this line, and they are now nearly or quite as safe, for they have a better foundation.

At Rochester we take seats in a long saloon-car. You enter at either end, through aisles with four state-rooms on each side, on one side for two persons, on the other for four. In the middle of the car is a saloon of twelve by nine feet and a half, with sofas well padded, and revolving easy-chairs. There is room in the car for fifty passengers, but half the seats are occupied. For the use of this car we pay about two-thirds of a cent per mile.

On our way east, we pass wheat, stubble, young orchards, corn and fields of broom-corn, pastures and meadows, and reach Albany by eight o'clock, P. M., and thence proceed by night car to Boston. We occupied in this car the last berth left, directly over the wheels, where the closets and wash-room are usually placed in the Pullman car, and here we were more jolted than on any portion of the line between the two oceans, although we caught a few hours' repose. We arrive in Boston at 6, A. M., on the morning of the 14th of September, after five weeks' absence.

I have thus given my diary for the trip, recording my observations and my sources of information, and here it gives me pleasure to tender to the officers of all the lines I have traversed, including Mr. Brydges, of the Grand Trunk, my acknowledgments for the facilities they have given, and the courtesies they have rendered.

I have made this tour with a view to ascertain the condition, capacity and resources of the lines which connect the Atlantic and the Pacific, and to embody the results in my Report. The weather has been favorable, my associates have aided me, and no source of information has been closed against me, and I now submit my conclusions.

Condition and Capacity of the Lines.

The Union and Central Pacific lines will soon be completed, but the finishing touch is yet to be given. Some abutments are to be renewed, some ballasting to be added, some temporary stations to be replaced with stone, some wooden bridges with iron; but the tracks are smooth and well laid, generally fish jointed; the alignment, in most cases, excellent; the gradients favorable, and the track so level and well sustained, that trains may run through the entire distance of eighteen hundred and sixty miles, from Omaha to Alameda, in the harbor of San Francisco, without fatigue to the traveller, in three days' time, or at the rate, including all stops and changes, of twenty-five miles per hour, and this too with sleeping cars on trains, whose dead weight exceeds a hundred and fifty tons, beside that of engine and tender, with cars which contain ample sleeping room for one hundred and forty passengers, and a restaurant and kitchen attached. Nor do I entertain any doubt that by the coming spring the roads might be run over by a light express train, as heavy as those between London and Liverpool, in two days, were it advisable to make such dispatch.

Connecting Lines.

The several lines running east from the Union Pacific to Chicago, have good curves and few changes of level; they require but little gravel and some new iron to enable trains to run regularly, in two days' time, between Omaha and the Atlantic cities of Philadelphia, New York, Boston and Montreal.

Cost of Running.

This depends chiefly on a few elements—the cost of fuel, ties, iron and wages. On the Pacific lines nature has been very beneficent. The coal at Carbon and Evanston, lies in close contiguity to the line, at the height of seven thousand feet above the sea, and about half way between Omaha and Sacramento; while wood abounds on the Sierra Nevada.

As Respects Road Repairs.

For seven-eights of the distance the climate is dry, and wood is enduring, and, in the language of the late James Hayward, "water is the great enemy of railways." On the Sierra and the Truckee river ties may be had at low prices. They are floated down the North Platte River, and will probably be delivered next year at Columbus, ninety-two miles west of Omaha, at the rate of sixty to seventy cents per tie.

When the road is finished with iron superstructures for its bridges, and sufficient ballast, five men can easily keep eight miles at grade.

As respects iron, a rolling mill may be placed at Carbon, and the defective rails sent through the rolls; and any new iron required is to be found near the railway, in the shape of magnetic iron ore.

Chinese track-men, quiet, docile and industrious, may be had for less than Eastern rates, or at thirty-five dollars per month. At these rates, and with eight trains running in each direction, by which the cost will be distributed, the cost of repairs will fall lightly, on each train mile. Until the line is finished and furnished with suitable bridges, and coal substituted for wood, the cost of repairs per train mile will be in excess, but will furnish no fair standard for the cost of running. Were we to measure the cost of fuel by the cost of wood, provided with undue haste for the extension of the line, and apply the present cost of keeping up the track, and of constructing perishable bridges in a dry climate, to two or three trains each way, we might possibly add a third to the necessary cost of running these Pacific railways.

But the advent of coal reduces the cost of fuel to ten or twelve cents per mile; the completion of track and bridges will reduce two-thirds the cost of road repairs for each mile run, and it is safe to predict that under judicious management the trains may be run eventually as cheaply as the trains on the Illinois Central line, or for less than one dollar and ten cents per mile.

Cost of Running on the Union Pacific.

The combination of favorable gradients with the possession of coal, the light fall of rain and snow, both of which are not equivalent to more than twelve inches of rain annually, conspire to lighten the cost of running on the Union Pacific, and that cost must fall with the increase of trains.

Cost on the Central Pacific.

This will probably exceed that on the Union, in consequence of higher gradients and the absence of coal, but the local business of the Central Pacific furnishes a compensation.

Comparative Condition of the Two Lines.

Union Pacific.

This line has a good alignment, bold curves and favorable gradients. The coal is found on it, and the most western mine is seventy miles east of Ogden.

Connecting with numerous lines, it has many feeders and some decided advantages over the Kansas Pacific, from greater facilities for reaching the lumber region and the navigable waters of the lakes.

According to my best judgment, ~~three~~ *two* millions of dollars, or ~~a million~~ less than it claims from the Central Pacific, will complete its bridges, ballast its line, complete its stations and make it one of the best, if not the best line, west of the Mississippi.

Central Pacific.

This line makes a favorable impression upon the traveller. Its road-bed is wide, it is well ballasted, its rail is in excellent condition, its equipage abundant. A few hundred thousand dollars will complete its surfacing and stations. It is possible that it might have avoided some undulations in its line, and have saved a few miles' distance, but there are few lines on which some improvements may not be made.

When the business of this line is more fully developed, and trains now light become heavy and shall be taken at low competing rates, policy will suggest some modifications of the route, but when we balance the cost of change and the interest on cost against advantages, changes that may be desirable in the future, may well be deferred.

As respects ties, the line has great resources in the lumber of the Sierra Nevada. It can command Chinese labor and resort to the rolling mills of San Francisco, for the renewal of its rails.

In the Sierra Nevada it will doubtless be its policy to introduce sections of iron into its snow-sheds, and at an early day to replace its trestle bridges with iron.

EQUIPAGE OF THE PACIFIC LINES.
Union Pacific.

The equipage of this line, as reported to us at Omaha, consists of one hundred and sixty engines, eighty passenger, mail and baggage cars, besides twenty Pullman cars, in which the line has an interest, and three thousand freight and gravel cars, some of which are now let for $11,000 monthly.

Central Pacific.

The equipage of this line, as reported by the officials, consists of one hundred and sixty-six engines and twenty-four engines ordered and in progress, one hundred and twenty-six passenger cars, twenty-four baggage and express cars, two thousand one hundred and seventy-four freight cars and ninety-five gravel cars.

The engines and cars are reported to be generally efficient and in good condition on both lines. Here is equipage sufficient to run eight trains daily in each direction, and less than three are now run. From the nature of the business, many of the trains must be fast trains, requiring few cars, and for the present the lines are apparently overstocked, and have made a more liberal provision of rolling stock than any American line I know of has made at the outset. Should the stock now on hand be all required, it would earn sufficient beyond interest on the capital and debt to pay for large additions, and I cannot see any reason for providing additional equipage, unless it be some more sleeping cars, and cars suitable for fish and fruit, and a few more snow-ploughs. Both lines, with respect to equipage, are first-class railways.

Provisions against Snow.

The experience of the Central Railway for several winters, while constructing the line over the Sierra Nevada, has led it to make liberal provisions of snow-sheds and safeguards against avalanches. The Union Pacific, with less snow on its line, is obliged to guard against a dry, drifting snow, which last winter gave it much annoyance, and for more than three weeks delayed its trains. To guard against such delays, it is of the highest importance that several cuts should be widened, several miles of snow-sheds thrown over cuts, and several snow-fences be erected. Materials for these have been collected, and plans made by General Dodge, who awaits orders. It is to be hoped that this work, in which the whole country is interested, will be at once completed.

Importance of Completing the Lines at once.

I am deeply impressed with the importance of completing both lines, as nearly as possible, the present autumn. If the work is done now, and charged at once to construction, it will have the best effect upon future net income. It will reduce the cost of road repairs, prevent the diversion of revenue into construction, to the injury of credit; it will prevent the possible loss of one or two millions of income by snow during the winter, and in all respects conduce to the interest and reputatation of the line.

The question at Promontory should be adjusted by agreement or reference. Ogden, or some point between Ogden and Corinne, is the true point for a junction, in accordance with the agreement of the parties.

Any branch to Montana or Oregon would, in the opinion of General Dodge, diverge at Granger, not Corinne, and ties and lumber floating down the Bear River may be easily taken from the river to a point near Ogden, by the lake.

While this question remains open, trains are delayed and passengers are incommoded, and each line may harm the other by unfriendly action.

This question, which springs from the energy and rivalry of each line, should be settled, and proper stations and waterworks erected at the point of junction.

Cost of Construction.

I am satisfied by my inquiries and observation, that the cost of the Union Pacific line has been greatly underrated by the public.

It is true that many sections of the railway are built on light embankments, across plains nearly level, but surveys have been expensive; there has been heavy work on the mountains and costly bridging and masonry and costly renewals of masonry. Large stations and long turnouts have been finished and a large and costly equipage provided. Bonds have been sold at a discount, transportation of materials has been costly and wages and provisions have been dear in the wilderness.

According to my best judgment, the loan from government will not more than suffice to cover the necessary cost of surveys, graduation, bridging and masonry, including the new work for bridges yet incomplete, the discount on bonds and the interest which has accumulated.

Nor will the money realized from the mortgage bonds, in my opinion, meet the cash cost of the superstructure, stations and equipage which must, with the transportation of the iron, exceed $30,000 a mile.

A part of the cost and of the amount paid in profits to contractors, must be drawn from the stock and land grant bonds.

Much of the iron on this line has probably cost $140 per ton in prime cost and transportation before it reached the track. Many of the ties have cost more than a dollar each on the track. Twenty thousand dollars a mile is a moderate estimate for the cost of track with turnouts, and ten thousand will be too low for stations and equipage, interest, discounts and general expenses, when the line is equipped. The officers of the line expect to meet the floating debt and finish the line, with their surplus property and claims.*

On the Central Pacific the stock is held by a few individuals, and it is supposed the government loan and an equal amount of mortgage bonds, less than fifty millions, together will nearly suffice to complete and equip the line of 700 miles from Ogden to Sacramento. What are the prospects of a return upon these investments?

* See Appendix.

Income.

The tracks of the two companies were connected at Promontory, on the tenth of May, and in May, June and July, 1869, passengers, mails, baggage, express and freight were transferred, and the revenue of each company for the three months was about two millions of dollars, drawn in great part from local business.

In August, the fast freight cars were sent through, but the through business thus far, has been chiefly experimental. By the tables, however, annexed to this Report, it will appear, that while the contractors' freight has diminished, the regular business of the line is steadily increasing, and is done at high rates with few trains.

The precise cost of doing the business cannot yet be defined, as the trains are run partly with wood and partly with cheap coal, and the officials and trackmen are engaged in completing the line; but if we estimate it at a dollar and forty cents a mile, in paper, which must greatly exceed the future cost, and assume that three trains are run daily, the running expenses of the Union Pacific for May, June and July, would not exceed $900,000, and leave sufficient to cover interest on all its loans for that period.

Earnings prior to Completion.

It would be politic for the line to charge interest to capital, until completion, and carry its net income drawn from unfinished sections to a reserve fund, to meet future casualties and deficiencies.

It will be its policy, also, to develop its business, now barely begun, as fast as possible, for the line is now ready for a much larger traffic than the present. It has barely touched its new sources of business.

Earnings of the Central Pacific.

This line already earns, from a track less in length than that of the Union Pacific, a gross revenue as large or larger than that of the Union Pacific. It is drawn in great part from local business.

As, however, the gradients are heavier, and coal will cost more on this line than on the other, the cost of transportation will somewhat exceed that of the Union Pacific; and as the through business increases, its returns to each line will be proportioned to its length, and we may expect a large accession to the population of the plains.

FUTURE SOURCES OF BUSINESS.

Fruit and fish should furnish a very important traffic to these lines; if the business is properly developed and proper facilities given, California, with fast trains and an exuberance of fruit, can furnish the Atlantic cities with choice pears, plums, apricots, melons and many vegetables earlier than they can be produced in the Atlantic States, and grapes that will not grow there except under glass.

Trains of ten or twelve cars, with fruit, emigrants and second-class passengers, should be sent through at a speed of twenty miles an hour. At six cents per pound, to all points beyond the Mississippi, such trains might earn four dollars per train mile and pay large profits, returning with merchandise at slow rates of speed.

Halibut, salmon and shell-fish might be sent at the same rates, with great profit, and butter, cheese, lard, lard-oil and hams, from the West, be taken as return freights.

But there are other and more important sources of profit. Tea, coffee, sugar, silk and spices. Most of these commodities can be landed at less prices on the Pacific coast than they can be on the Atlantic. For instance, fifty million pounds of tea are sent from China and Japan to New York and Boston, for fifteen dollars per measurement ton; but if we add to this the interest and insurance, and other charges, the cost of the transit is about six cents per pound in currency.

A fair freight by ships from Shanghai to San Francisco would be but five dollars per measurement ton, and as the distance is little more than one-third of that to New York, tea might be laid down in the port of San Francisco for less than two and a half cents per pound, which would give San Francisco an advantage of more than three cents over New York. At a freight of two and a half cents a pound, by railway, it would not only reach New York, but might go through to Europe and the British Provinces.*

As respects sugar, coffee, spices and Manilla grass, the importations of the United States now approach a million of tons, and these articles from Asia, the Asiatic and the Sandwich Isles, can be landed in San Francisco at less cost than at New York, if we take into account the fact that silver and flour can be best shipped from San Francisco in payment.

With this advantage, and a freight of two and a half cents per pound, the imports from San Francisco would meet those from New York in the basin of the Mississippi, and the Pacific lines might well compete with the lines from the Atlantic, and reasonably expect to attract capital to California, and to carry one-third of these imports.

Again, these Pacific lines might attract several thousand tons of raw silk from China, and shoes and dry goods from the East, at very high prices, and carry wool and wine at third-class rates. Already the Isthmus line is transporting hides, wool and other California freight to New York, at $1\frac{1}{2}$ cents per pound in gold, and if we add to this the premium on gold, insurance and interest, we bring the rate to $2\frac{1}{2}$ cents per pound. It is unquestionably the policy of the Pacific railways to induce the owners of the line *via* the Isthmus to transfer two-thirds of their steamers from Aspinwall and Panama, to the China line. Such a change, and it is already foreshadowed by the withdrawal of a monthly steamer from the Isthmus route, would add at least three millions to the income of the railways.

* See Appendix.

It may be urged that 2½ cents per pound, or $50 per ton, would not pay, but the propellers and great lines to Chicago carry their fourth-class freight one-third of that distance for $7 to $10 per ton, or at half the rate per mile here proposed. It will be an object to them to encourage this traffic, and I do not hesitate to recommend to the Pacific lines to send freight to all points east of the Mississippi for the following rates: Six cents per pound for first-class fast freight; five cents per pound for general merchandise; two and a half cents for third-class, to include domestic goods and groceries.

Tariff.

It is of the greatest importance that the rates should at once be fixed, and that publicity be given to them. It may be that at somewhat higher rates of freight than those suggested, some business may be done with the interior, but it appears to me that the rates I have recommended will develop a great traffic; will compete with the Isthmus line, divert its steamers to the China line, and meet the expectations of the country. I would also, without disturbing the local rates, or rates for emigrants, recommend the directors to consider the policy of reducing the rates on first-class passengers and of establishing second-class rates, and restaurants on the line, where the common articles of food may be had at moderate prices. At present the steamers *via* the Isthmus furnish food and lodging for their passengers of all classes, which are not furnished by the railways.

Propellers to China.

It seems to me very desirable, also, to secure the establishment of a line of propellers between San Francisco and China. They will find a profitable trade in tea, sugar, rice, silk, spices, and in Chinese emigrants, going and returning. In flour and rice and domestics, they may often make good freights, and may also make a percentage on silver.

Steamers are now built on the Clyde, which carry a thousand tons of freight, with an expenditure of but ten tons of coal in twenty-four hours on the rough billows of the Atlantic.

The present line to China, giving but one steamer a month, and charging $15 per measurement ton for tea, and running in connection with the Isthmus line, does not meet at all the requirements of the railways.

Chinese.

These Asiatics have made themselves very acceptable in California, to all but those classes of foreigners whose labor they compete with. They will be of great value to the capitalists who would build railways or open copper mines, or extend the garden cultivation of California, and very useful on the Southern plantations. It is estimated in London that ten thousand a month might be easily induced to emigrate from China. They are content with little, and in five years might accumulate sufficient to take them back and make them happy in their native land. Such a stream of travel, coming and returning, would enrich the railways, and deserves every encouragement.

Express.

I learn with great satisfaction that both railways have agreed to pursue a course I have long advocated, viz., to take the express business into their own hands. I found several instances at points on the route to the Atlantic, where dealers desired to order fruit from California, but were deterred by the express charges of twenty to twenty-four cents per pound. I found, too, the express company took, in my own case, six days to do what could easily have been done in two. Such charges and such neglect would be disastrous to the fruit trade, and check the progress of the railways, and will, it is hoped, soon be ended.

The specie alone, passing over these lines, should pay the two railways sixty thousand dollars a month.

Telegraph.

Another source of income is the telegraph. The two railways now hold a telegraph line with two wires, by which they guide their operations, but from which they derive no income, and I am informed that the Western Union Company earns more than thirty thousand dollars a month from their parallel line to the Atlantic States, at charges of $6 to $7 for a single message.

Competition may reduce prices, but will stimulate business, and there is little doubt that the railways, as trade quickens, may draw from this source a revenue of fifteen to twenty thousand dollars a month.

Value of Land.

The Union Pacific line holds a large body of land, granted by the government to encourage the enterprise. The land agent, Mr. Davis, after making allowance for prior sales, pre-emptions and Indian reservations, estimates this grant to cover twelve million of acres, and it seems to me rates it low at a dollar and a half per acre, as it lies within the average distance of ten miles from the railway.

For two hundred miles from Omaha, the land is very fertile and well adapted to agriculture; beyond this is a district apparently designed for stock farms, in most of which cattle and sheep winter in the open air. A large portion of the more remote lands show indications of alkali, and for many miles coal shows itself; while iron ore of good quality is found in considerable quantities.

The Alkali Country.

In the vast territories of Wyoming, Utah and Nevada, crossed by the Pacific railways, the traveller notices large areas covered with sage bush and brown grasses, and often with an efflorescence or crust, resembling the ice cakes on salt marshes. This is the alkali country, and here one often finds no pure water or food for man or beast, and comes to the conclusion that the country is a waste, and doomed to perpetual sterility.

Meanwhile the Mormon and the Californian have opened wheat fields, orchards and vineyards in lands containing alkali in greater or less degrees, and by artificial or natural irrigation have converted the waste into a garden.

Is it safe to pronounce such a country sterile and irreclaimable? The brown grasses nourished the elk and the buffalo.

A careful analysis of the alkali of the plains resolves it into salt, soda, potash, lime and magnesia; most of the salts it contains are conducive to fertility, and they are combined with ammonia and carbonic acid, both essential to the growth of vegetation.

Liebig, the great chemist of Europe, in his "Treatise on Chemistry applied to Agriculture," reports each of these salts as essential to fertile soils, and sterility is due to their absence.

He finds them diminishing in the ashes of the tobacco plant as the soil becomes exhausted; he traces them in the ashes of the wheat, barley and oat plant, in diminishing proportions, as we descend from wheat to oats.

He discovers them as the components of the ashes of horse manure and of guano, and finds them most abundant in the ashes of trees with deciduous leaves.

Here, then, we have in the alkali the great agents of fertility, sufficient not only to fertilize the soil they cover, but to enrich other districts, and to contribute to arts and manufactures. Here is a field for the directing mind of America and for the patient industry of Asia in the coming centuries, in guiding the rill from snow-clad mountains to thirsty plains; in lifting water by artesian wells or by windmills or engines from lake and river, and in applying it to animate nature, and to set in motion her elements of fertility. And nature will respond to the call of humanity. Each orchard planted will bring down showers from heaven and double the effects of man's exertions.

I feel convinced the value of the alkali land is greatly underrated, and that the estimate of Mr. Davis, which he thinks a low one, is very moderate.

Land of the Central Pacific Railroad Company.

The lands of this company differ from those of the Union Pacific. Instead of forming plains like those of the Platte, they commence near the foot-hills and rise rapidly on the sides of the Sierra, and then extend across basins encircled by mountains, and rise to an elevation of four to seven thousand feet above the sea.

The portion on the Sierra is quite valuable for its pine timber; the timber land differs from that of Maine, where a few pines are found in clusters among maple, birch and spruce trees. Here many large pines are found growing together, and the land is heavily timbered with trees fit for the saw-mill.

The Central Pacific line has about eight million acres. Much of it is alkali land, much fit for pasturage. It probably would not sell at present for more than five millions, but may eventually command a much higher price.

Comparisons with other Lines.

If we compare the cost of the Pacific lines with those of Massachusetts, we find the average cost for the last is $72,000 per mile; and if we deduct the inferior lines, we shall find some of the chief railways of the States have cost as much as the Pacific lines, and are at a high premium.

The Illinois Central line, in some particulars, resembles the Pacific lines, although its cost is less. It received a land grant of 2,595,000 acres from the United States. It commenced running with a length of 708 miles in 1856. Its capital stock was then $8,258,615. Its debt, $19,841,724. Its equipage but 91 engines and 1,690 cars.

Its gross earnings in 1856 were	$2,476,035 00
Its running expenses,	1,444,546 00
Its net income,	$1,031,489 00
Deducting State tax,	93,052 00
The balance of income was but	$938,437 00

But one-third of the line was entirely ballasted.
From this feeble beginning it has advanced, until, in 1868,—

Its stock has increased to	$25,277,270 00
Its debt diminished to	9,377,500 00
Its earnings, from Illinois lines, increased to	6,797,930 00

With all this success, its revenue is but $1\frac{05}{100}$ per train mile, and its cost of running $1\frac{2}{100}$ per train mile.

The aggregate sales of its land to 1869 have been $22,122,830, with one-fourth of its land unsold. The receipts from land have nearly equalled the original cost of the line.

The dividend has reached eighteen per cent., and in twelve years the revenue has tripled. In 1856 it was but four per cent. on the cost of the line. The land unsold will pay the residue of its debt. The position of the Pacific lines, in several respects, is more favorable. Their rates are much higher, and their receipts per mile of road are much larger, at the completion of their enterprise, than those of the Illinois Central Railway.

If we compare the returns of the Pacific railways with those of the Grand Trunk line for 1867 and 1868, we find, on the

Grand Trunk Railway, that its freight trains have averaged 17 cars; its passenger trains, 5 cars. Its cost of running has been, without coal, and with wood at $4.00 per cord, $\frac{99}{100}$ of a cent per mile. Its average earnings per hundred miles,—from each passenger, $1.06; from each ton of freight, 86 cents. Expense of each passenger for 100 miles, 85 cents; expense of each ton of freight, 65 cents. Net earnings per ton and per passenger for 100 miles, 21 cents. Gross earnings of 1,377 miles, $7,000,000.

These earnings, long subsequent to the opening of the line, are much below those of the Pacific lines, on which the net profit is much higher.

Conclusion.

The rates I have recommended are in currency, but they will gradually advance as the country returns to gold by the improvement of the currency, and will meanwhile have developed business.

No one can visit California and observe the progress that country has made in the last ten years under a specie currency, in its agriculture, mines, manufactures, trade, banks, buildings and the value of property, without being impressed with the importance of an early return to a specie basis.

Without it, what assurance have we that Messrs. Fisk and Gould may not again disturb values as they did last week in New York? Why should Congress or our courts demoralize the country, now that the crisis has passed, by debasing our standard of values? Why should thousands of men be diverted from agriculture and the mechanic arts to bet upon the price of gold and to get up false rumors? The return to gold will minister to the prosperity of the Pacific railways.

In this Report I have endeavored to do justice to both of the great lines to the Pacific, and cannot close it without commending the spirit and energy with which they have been driven to a successful consummation.

In the last three years a herculean feat has been accomplished. In that brief period at least fifteen hundred miles of railway have been carried through the wilderness. If there has been a large expenditure incurred, we must not forget that seven years' interest on unproductive outlay has been avoided, and the march of improvement has been accelerated.

I have also endeavored to give the distinctive features and merits of the Union and Central Pacific lines.

If they are properly finished and managed, as I believe they will be, in the liberal spirit the country has a right to expect, I venture to foretell that they will requite the nation for its favors, meet the wishes of the public and the hopes of their stockholders, and I predict for them a brilliant future.

I have the honor to be,

Very sincerely,

E. H. DERBY.

APPENDIX.

[No. 1.]

While this report was in the hands of a copyist, I made a short excursion to the White Mountains of New Hampshire. While there I met a very intelligent man, who had resided for many years near the line of the Grand Trunk Railway in Northern New Hampshire, and he gave me the following exhibit of its condition:

"Its road-bed is good and its bridges excellent and its engine-"men and firemen equal to any in the States. Its track between "Gorham and Portland for ninety miles has been renovated and "two-thirds of it laid with new iron. Last year the State authori-"ties restricted it to twelve miles an hour; this year the passenger "trains run twenty-two miles the hour. From Gorham to Mon-"treal the track is single and requires renewal. How could it be "otherwise, when it sends twenty-four heavy trains daily over a "single track, and most of its iron has been down many years."

"There have been many delays and accidents on this line of "late years. At one time several trains were off the track at once, "and the chief business of the county courts is to try suits for "damages and detention against the Grand Trunk. It has been "the policy of the directors to discharge the Americans in the "management and to put on dispatch agents and other officials "who are foreigners and hold themselves aloof from the citizens on "the line. They are of course out of favor, and when men sue it, "the road suffers in damages and costs.

"A few months since, the cars ran through a flock of sheep—"the owner would have settled for those killed, at two dollars each, "and the jury gave him twelve dollars a head.

"A lawyer called on an official to ascertain why his client's "freight was detained. He was ill-treated and brought a suit for "the insult; before trial he was appointed judge, and the jury "made the road pay him four thousand dollars for the insult.

"As respects wood, the line runs much of the way in Maine and "New Hampshire through forests, and wood is worth, for soft "wood but fifty cents and for hard wood but seventy-five cents per "cord, standing. It costs but $1.00 to have it cut by Canadians "and but $1.00 to $1.25 to have it hauled, so that it costs but $2.50 "to $3.00 per cord, delivered on the line of the road. At this rate "any quantity desired could be purchased, but the road pays $4.00 "to $4.50 per cord, and some one makes a profit. The road agent "instead of contracting in each township for the wood required "there, invites proposals for all the wood wanted on the whole "length in the United States.

"Few can propose for so large an amount, and if they did, would "probably propose in vain.

"As respects revenue, the principal freight of the road is lumber. "Spruce boards have risen in the last ten years from $6.00 in gold "to $15.00 in paper, per thousand, at the mills. The freight, "formerly $3.00 a thousand in gold, is now $3.00 a thousand in "paper and might be increased, for the mills are making money. "One town sends to Portland some sixteen million feet of boards."

These at $6.00 per thousand, would add $48,000 to the net income of the line and would pay for one or two hundred miles, better than flour at a dollar a barrel for a thousand miles from Toronto to Halifax.

These representations must pass for what they are worth. To point out such evils is to suggest the remedy.

It is not easy for Englishmen, in the opinion of my informant, to run the line successfully in the United States. With half a million sterling expended between Portland and Sarnia and American managers, east of Canada, the line would soon make returns.

Last year, the crops on the line were deficient. This year the bountiful harvests will be of service to the line, which will now have an improved connection with Chicago, and should form one of the routes from Europe, the Lower Provinces, Portland, Montreal and Boston to San Francisco, *via* the Union and Central Pacific Railways.

[No. 2.]

Earnings of the Union Pacific Railway Company, as furnished by the Boston Office.

1869.	Passengers.	Freight.	Express and Miscellaneous.	Mails.	Troops and Freight. Government.	Men and Material. Contractors.	Totals.
May 10th to 31st,	$216,607 18	$127,224 31	$17,487 34	$16,589 29	$106,689 04	$106,752 96	$591,420 12
June,	331,099 12	197,908 55	48,014 99	23,229 17	70,778 64	34,672 22	706,002 29
July,	329,358 20	173,079 13	23,618 21	23,229 17	63,024 62	10,320 63	623,559 96
August,	367,197 85	143,192 73	25,424 65	24,828 53	56,026 82	911 80	617,585 38
September,	475,302 12	194,965 04	20,000 00*	22,911 00	51,906 75	—	765,084 91

* Estimated.

It was also stated to me at Omaha, that the surplus cars were yielding $11,000 a month. I have also received from the Boston office the following statement of the capital and debt of the Union Pacific,

Government Bonds,	$26,638,000 00
First Mortgage Bonds,	29,000,000 00
Land Grant Bonds,	10,000,000 00
Capital Stock issued,	29,762,000 00

To this must be added a small floating debt and the cost of completing the line, which, it is hoped, may be covered by the surplus assets of the company. A portion of the government bonds, about two and one-third millions, are yet to be delivered to the Company.

[No. 3.]

October 12th, 1869.

A letter from R. W. Woodbury, Esq., Secretary of the Denver Board of Trade, apprises me that in 1868, 15,000 head of cattle were driven from Colorado across the mountains to California, after having been fattened in Colorado, where the grass is more nutritious than it is in New Mexico.

The present value of cattle in Colorado is 3½ cents per pound on the hoof. About forty thousand head of cattle will be shipped either in beef or alive this autumn from Colorado to Chicago, over the Union Pacific line, and the rate paid for 500 miles on the Union Pacific, from Cheyenne to Omaha, will be $240 per carload.

One man ships 20,000 head of slaughtered cattle. The freight on the Union Pacific line will be not far from $400,000 on the forty thousand head of cattle.

[No. 4.]

Michigan Central Railway.

Business in 1860 and in 1869.

	Gross Earnings.	Tons Moved.	Passengers.	Net Receipts.
1860, . . .	$1,832,945 00	295,276	324,421	$755,461 00
1869, . . .	4,716,293 00	802,835	846,452	1,829,349 00

In 1860 the gross earnings were less than $7,000 per mile a year, or less per mile a week than those of the Pacific lines since their opening. The Michigan Central Railway was opened as early as 1847.

The Overland Route to the Pacific. 93

Its earnings per ton a mile were, in the year ending May 31, 1869,—

On through freight, ...	1 $\frac{51}{100}$ cts.
On local freight, ...	3 $\frac{52}{100}$
Average, ...	2 $\frac{3}{100}$ cts.

The president of this successful company, Mr. Joy, remarks, in his report :—

"In view of the rapid development of the country, and espec-
"ially of the progressive and rapid settlement of the West, and
"vast increase of its productions, depending upon cheap transpor-
"tation for their value, the great aim of railway companies should
"be to so perfect their roads and appointments as to transact the
"immense business of the country at the least possible expense,
"and rely upon the volume of business to be done at reasonable
"rates, rather than upon smaller amounts, with higher charges.

"The reduction of through passenger fares during the past year
"has been one-fifth, and perhaps that of the rates of through
"freight has been nearly in proportion."

[No. 5.]

NATIONAL LOAN.

The Act establishing the Union Pacific Railway Company, (Acts of 1862, chapter 120, section 5,) provides that the six per cent. bonds issued in aid of the same, shall be payable thirty years after date; and, "that to secure the repayment to the United States, as "thereinafter provided, of the amount of said bonds, so issued and "delivered to said company, together with all interest thereon which "shall have been paid by the United States, the issue of said bonds "and delivery to the company shall, *ipso facto*, constitute a first "mortgage on the whole line of the railroad and telegraph, together "with the rolling stock, fixtures and property, of every kind and

"description, and in consideration of which, said bonds may be
"issued, and on the refusal or failure of said company to redeem said
"bonds, or any part of them when required so to do by the Secre-
"tary of the Treasury, in accordance with the provisions of this act,
"the said road, with all the rights, functions, immunities and appur-
"tenances thereto belonging, and also all lands granted to said com-
"pany by the United States, which at the time of said default shall
"remain in the ownership of said company, may be taken possession
"of by the Secretary of the Treasury for the use and benefit of the
"United States."

Section 6 of the same Act provides "that the grants to said com-
"pany are made upon condition that said company shall pay said
"bonds at maturity, and shall keep the line in repair and transmit
"mails, troops, stores and munitions for the government at all times,
"giving them the preference, at fair and reasonable rates, and that
"all compensation for services rendered to the government shall be
"applied to the payment of said bonds and interest until the whole
"is paid, and that after the railroad is finished five per cent. of its
"net income, in addition, shall be applied to the reduction of inter-
"est and principal of the loan of the United States."

By section 5, chapter 216 of the Acts of the United States for 1864, it is provided that "but one-half of the compensation for ser-
"vices shall be applied towards the payment of the principal and
"interest of said government bonds."

By section 10 of the Act last named, precedence is given to the mortgage bonds of the company over the mortgage to the United States for an amount equal to the amount of government bonds.

It is further provided by said Acts, that the companies building said roads may unite and form one company; and by chapter 88 of Acts of 1865, the Union Pacific and Central Pacific Railroad Cos. are empowered to make the interest on these bonds for thirty years, payable in any lawful currency of the United States.

It would appear from these provisions that the United States have, by their Acts in aid, given precedence to the first mortgage bonds of the company, over those issued by the United States, and that the latter are to be paid at maturity, and if they are not then paid, with all interest accrued, the United States may enter upon the property, and that two provisions are made for the payment of interest, viz., by an appropriation of one-half the amount required for services rendered to the United States, and five per cent. of the net income of the company, after the railway is completed.

In case these should not suffice to meet the interest, the Acts appear to contain no express provision for an entry for non-payment of interest until the bonds mature.

The Acts seem carefully drawn to protect the company in its infancy, and the United States, which by this railway reduces the cost of transportation of troops, stores and mails across the plains, more than eighty per cent., can well afford to continue their liberality and to wait for a part of their interest.

As population becomes more dense on the line, the services required by the government, and the net income of the company, will increase, and with it the proceeds of the percentage will grow also. When the net income exceeds ten per cent., the United States, under the provisions of the Acts, may again intervene, and reduce the tariff.

[No. 6.]

October 7th, 1869.

One of the principal dealers in tea in Boston informs me that the Souchong tea, which forms the principal part of the tea imported into the United States, comes in chests which measure five cubic feet, eight of which constitute a measurement ton. These chests weigh 115 pounds each, including the tea. The tare or weight of the chest is rated by the trade at 25 pounds to the chest, and the net weight of the tea is 90 pounds, or 720 pounds of tea to the measurement ton. At the customary freight of $16 per measurement ton from Shanghai to Boston, the cost would be $2\frac{22}{100}$ cents per pound.

To this we must add for interest and insurance five per cent., and for commissions and discount on bills of exchange three per cent., which last item may possibly be saved by the remittance of silver from San Francisco, which derives a supply of at least ten millions of silver yearly from the mines of Nevada.

Assuming the average cost of tea at 28 cents a pound in China, the interest, insurance and discount, viz., 8 per cent., would amount to $2\frac{24}{100}$ cents; and if we add this to the freight, the aggregate cost would amount to $4\frac{2}{3}$ cents from Shanghai to Boston in gold; and if we add a third to convert this into currency, the entire cost of the importation in currency is $6\frac{23}{100}$ cents per pound.

The freight and charges by sailing vessel to San Francisco on the Pacific for two-fifths of the distance from Shanghai to Boston should not exceed three cents a pound; and thus San Francisco will be able to compete for the trade from China to the Atlantic ports, if the charge by railway does not exceed two and a half cents per pound, and the tea is transferred from the ship to the car without injury.

[No. 7.]

A new Fastening or Substitute for Chairs and Fish-Joints.

Since my return, I have recently examined a new fastening for the joints of rails, which has been adopted and improved on the Fitchburg and Boston and Providence Railways, which gives great satisfaction, and is found to be altogether superior to the common fish-joint.

On these railways, chairs are now dispensed with, and the ┬ rail, with a flat base, is so laid, that the joint is suspended between two ties or sleepers, two feet apart, measuring from centre to centre. Under the joint is placed a shoe, two feet long, of half-inch wrought iron, an inch or more wider than the base of the rail, with half an inch or more turned up on each side.

This shoe is perforated by two holes on each side, through which four bolts are driven into the ties. Above the joint, resting on the top of the base of the rails, two small plates of iron are placed, one on each side of the rails, which are connected by a bolt, in the shape of the letter U, which passes through the plates and through crescents in the rails, one head coming up on each side, and the plates are screwed down with head-screws, to hold the bottom of the rail in place.

Some of these fastenings have been in use for years, and the substitution of them for chairs and fish-plates is thought to add a third to the life of the tie.

Mr. Stearns, of the Fitchburg line, has also increased the strength and durability of his rails by raising their height half an inch, without increasing their weight.

[No. 8.]

OCTOBER 22, 1869.

While revising the proof of this Report, I learn from the office of the Union Pacific that a new weekly train, with Pullman cars and a hotel car attached, commenced this week to run between Omaha and San Francisco, and will make the trip in eighty-one hours, stopping for wood and water only. Passengers desirous to take this train may engage their berths by telegram, and travel by any route to Omaha, stopping or not on the way. They may thus pass a day or two at any of the cities between the seaboard and the Union Pacific, or go through in about fifty hours to Omaha. I am also apprised that the earnings of the Union Pacific continue to grow, and were, for the first fifteen days of October, $412,024.53, or at the rate of ten million dollars per annum for one thousand and ninety-one miles. There is reason to hope the expenses may fall below forty per cent., as the business is done with few trains and at remunerative rates.

www.ingramcontent.com/pod-product-compliance
Lightning Source LLC
Chambersburg PA
CBHW031122160426
43192CB00008B/1086